THE
FLOUR CRAFT
BAKERY & CAFÉ COOKBOOK

THE
FLOUR CRAFT
BAKERY & CAFÉ COOKBOOK

Inspired Gluten-Free Recipes for
Breakfast, Lunch, Tea & Celebrations

HEATHER HARDCASTLE

Photographs by Erin Scott

RIZZOLI
NEW YORK

New York · Paris · London · Milan

For Rick, my best friend and partner in life and work. This book simply would not be possible without your tireless support and encouragement. I'm beyond lucky to call you "my person."

The Flour Craft Bakery & Café Cookbook
by Heather Hardcastle

First published in 2021 in the United States of America by
Rizzoli International Publications, Inc.
300 Park Avenue South
New York, NY 10010
rizzoliusa.com

Photography and prop styling by Erin Scott
erinscottstudio.com
Food styling by Lillian Kang
mrsmochi.com

Publisher: Charles Miers
Editor: Jono Jarrett
Design: Ashley Lima
Production Manager: Colin Hough-Trapp
Managing Editor: Lynn Scrabis

Printed in China
2021 2022 2023 2024 / 10 9 8 7 6 5 4 3 2 1

ISBN: 978-1-59962-159-3
Library of Congress Call Number: 2020941313

Visit us online:
Facebook.com/RizzoliNewYork
Twitter: @Rizzoli_Books
Instagram.com/RizzoliBooks
Pinterest.com/RizzoliBooks
Youtube.com/user/RizzoliNY

TABLE OF CONTENTS

INTRODUCTION

Baking is rich in history and tradition, it is full of possibility for experimentation, it is inherently creative, and it is something that when done well makes everyone happy, including the baker. I have always been drawn to a good challenge and to those pursuits that seem impossible to master, and launching my own gluten-free baking business falls squarely into that category. Starting something from nothing and learning as I go has just always made sense to me. I'd rather try and fail, which as a cook you do on a daily basis, rather than live with regret for not having tried at all.

My first passion was horses. I am, and always have been, obsessed with horses and all things to do with equestrian sports. Working with a large animal with its own distinctive personality presents a unique opportunity for learning and developing sensitivity. When you're riding a horse, you must delicately adapt in the moment to a constantly changing and potentially dangerous situation, a process that's very similar to the challenge of running a small business and working in a dynamic environment like a kitchen.

Always a reader, I loved to go to the bookstore. On one visit when I was ten, I came across John Robbins's Diet for a New America among the new releases in the food section. I was instantly hooked and insisted

on buying it with my own money. I devoured it within a week and announced that I was becoming a vegetarian from that moment forward. My parents said if that was the case, I had better start learning to cook as they had no idea what to feed me. I took that challenge seriously and have been experimenting with food and cooking ever since. While I currently do eat some fish and seafood, I have been a vegetarian for many years. You'll notice all the recipes in this book have integrity as vegetarian recipes, without the use of meat as a primary ingredient. Some recipes do include fish like smoked salmon or trout but the decision to add it or skip it is entirely yours. I encourage you to add other animal proteins, should that feel right for you, but the recipes are complete on their own.

I'm a maker by nature and am drawn to tangible pursuits, things I can create with my own two hands. I came to cooking and baking later in life than most chefs, after having a decade-long career as a garden designer. My love for plants and combining them in beautiful and creative ways was art for me, with each environment presenting its own unique set of challenges. As with designing gardens, baking and the pursuit of perfection in something that will never be perfect is what kept me coming back for more.

There was always something new to learn and that depth of possibility was something I could really sink my teeth into.

And then, more than 20 years ago, I discovered I was gluten-intolerant. After a lifetime of digestive issues and perpetual discomfort after eating, I sought out the help of a nutritionist to get my health back on track. That realization was a complete game-changer for me. The gluten-free landscape then looked very different than it does now; it was still the "dark ages of gluten-free," as I call it. There were very few products available and those that I could find were hardly worth eating. I became passionate about baking at this time, determined to recreate the items I missed most, like a crusty sourdough bread or a simple apple pie with a flaky crust. I love sharing food with others, and seeing someone's eyes light up when I present them with a plate of homemade cookies or a freshly baked cake. Unwilling to accept the substandard gluten-free options available in stores, I decided to create my own.

Ten-plus years into my garden design career, and several years into serious gluten-free baking at home, I was itching for a new challenge. I loved working with plants yet would live for the weekends when I could be alone in my small home kitchen, cooking and baking. I decided it was time that I follow my passion and, in 2008, I enrolled in the Culinary Institute of America at Greystone,

in Napa Valley. I happily immersed myself in the baking world, gluten and all, and in doing so learned quickly that it was not something I could sustain in my new career. Just working with the flour gave me severe eczema, tasting bites of gluten-containing baked goods even in very small doses gave me terrible stomach pain that lasted for days. But I loved the work! The creativity of it all, the rich tradition of techniques, the endless opportunities for adaptation, and the constant challenges presented by working in such an intense environment resonated with me like nothing else ever had before.

After graduation, I took my newfound passion for baking, along with the basic techniques I had learned in cooking school, and began experiments in my own kitchen. Soon I had developed a successful gluten-free granola business, on which Flour Craft brick-and-mortar was eventually built. The experience of working the graveyard shift in a shared commercial kitchen with my husband Rick and selling our granola at a weekly farmers market showed me there was true enthusiasm for what we were making. I slowly introduced gluten-free pastries to our booth one by one, testing them on our loyal customers. Gaining confidence and perfecting my recipes in this environment was essential to honing the brand and led to the opening of our first retail location in 2013.

Since starting my food journey I've learned volumes. Running a restaurant is definitely not for the faint of heart. And for those of you who think otherwise, being a professional chef is anything but glamorous. I wash plenty of dishes, regularly scrub floor drains, clean out refrigerators, and work the line when someone calls out sick. Whatever is needed to support the business and my team is what I do. After all, working in a restaurant is the ultimate team sport and it takes everyone working in perfect unison for it to thrive. It's hard work, requires long hours, and is very physical but it's my passion. There is nothing else I'd rather do. And at the end of the day, I know it's time and energy well spent.

As Flour Craft continues to grow and evolve, I often think about what my next steps will be and how I can continue to push the boundaries of food and creativity. For me, cooking and baking is the ultimate lifelong learning pursuit. There is always something new to discover, whether it's a new ingredient, flavor combination, or technique. Lately my experiments have been focused around gluten-free sourdough and how to use it in unexpected sweet and savory applications to not only provide flavor, but great texture and health benefits as well. Having a platform from which to experiment and a willing group of testers (my loyal customers!) provides me with the ultimate satisfaction. Making food for others is my true calling.

It's how I express my love most easily to my family and friends. And each meal I make at the Flour Craft cafés is an extension of that for me. Food made with love tastes better. It just does.

In 2018, Rick and I opened our second retail location in Mill Valley, where we offer an expanded plant-forward savory menu in addition to the baked goods we have always been known for. I aim to share our repertoire from that entire evolution here, from Flour Craft classics to new inspirations for both sweet and savory recipes you can make for those you love. I hope this book inspires you to bring a taste of the Flour Craft community home and integrate that experience into your daily life. There is nothing that would bring me more joy. Happy baking!

TEATIME LOAVES

Lemon Drizzle Cake

Pistachio Pound Cake

Chocolate & Vanilla Marbled Pound Cake

Cocoa Nib Cream

Pumpkin Walnut Bread with Cream Cheese Icing

LEMON DRIZZLE CAKE

This simple drizzle cake is a favorite of anyone who loves lemon desserts. It has a good puckery, lemon kick and a buttery finish. The texture is irresistible, both dense and rich, like a proper pound cake should be. The lemon drizzle makes the cake super moist and gives it the ability to last for several days in the fridge, so it's perfect for making well ahead. It's excellent for dessert served with berries and unsweetened whipped cream or great on its own with an afternoon cup of tea.

MAKES ONE 9-INCH LOAF; COOK TIME: 55–60 MINUTES

FOR THE CAKE:

Butter, soft	10 oz / ½ cup plus 2 TB
White sugar	7 oz / 1 cup
Vanilla extract	2 tsp
Lemon zest	2 tsp
Eggs	5 large
Brown rice flour	5.5 oz / 1 cup
Millet flour	2.5 oz / ½ cup
Tapioca starch	3 oz / ⅓ cup
Kosher salt	½ tsp
Xanthan gum	¾ tsp
Baking powder	1 tsp
Whole milk	3 oz / ⅓ cup

FOR THE LEMON DRIZZLE:

Lemon juice	4 oz / ½ cup, from 2–3 lemons
White sugar	3.5 oz / ½ cup

1 Make the cake: Preheat the oven to 350°F. In the bowl of a stand mixer fitted with the paddle attachment, cream together butter and sugar on high speed until light and fluffy, about 3 minutes. Using a spatula, scrape down the sides of the bowl. Add vanilla and lemon zest and mix on medium speed for 1–2 minutes to combine.

2 With the mixer running on low speed, add eggs, one at a time, waiting until each egg is fully incorporated before adding the next. Scrape down the sides of the bowl once or twice between additions. Increase speed to medium and mix for 2–3 minutes until the eggs are fully incorporated into the mixture. It should look smooth and be a pale yellow color.

3 Add brown rice flour, millet flour, tapioca starch, salt, xanthan gum, and baking powder to the bowl and mix on low speed to combine. Scrape down the bottom and sides of the bowl, making sure to incorporate any bits of unmixed butter and sugar.

4 With the machine running on low, slowly pour in the milk. Increase mixer speed to high and continue mixing for 2 minutes until the batter is very light in color, smooth, and fluffy.

CONTINUED

5 Spray your loaf pan with cooking spray. Empty the batter into the pan, smoothing out the top with a spatula and taking care to spread the mixture evenly to the sides of the pan. Cover with foil and bake for 40 minutes. Remove the foil and bake for another 15–20 minutes, until the cake springs back when gently pushed with your finger and is a medium-gold color around the edges.

6 While the cake is baking, make the lemon drizzle: Heat the lemon juice in a small saucepan or in the microwave until very hot but not boiling. Whisk in the sugar until it is fully dissolved and no granules remain. Dissolving the sugar in the hot lemon juice will allow it to fully soak into the cake without crystallizing on the top. I like to make the drizzle while the cake is baking but you can make it well ahead of time, keep it in the fridge, and reheat it before pouring it onto the cake. If you do so, remember to whisk again to fully dissolve any sugar that may have re-crystallized.

7 When the cake is done allow it to cool on a rack for a few minutes in the pan then gently pierce it all over the top with a fork or a skewer, going about 2 inches deep. Pour the lemon drizzle over the surface of the cake, allowing it to soak into the top and run down the sides, between the cake and the pan. Let the cake rest about 30 minutes longer in the pan, then unmold it onto a baking sheet or cooling rack to cool completely. Allowing the cake to cool in the pan almost entirely will give time for the lemon drizzle to absorb completely into the cake and it will release more easily from the pan when you're ready to unmold it. Wrapped tightly in plastic wrap, the cake keeps well in the refrigerator for up to 1 week or in the freezer up to 1 month. Defrost at room temperature overnight before serving.

PISTACHIO POUND CAKE

This lovely, buttery cake is a delectable twist on a basic pound cake. The pistachios give it a pleasing, crunchy texture that pairs beautifully with the rich density of the cake itself. Pistachios also lend a fantastic vibrant green color to the interior of the cake that is a surprise when you cut it, as the top appears golden brown as it bakes. Fresh, unroasted, unsalted nuts that are bright green when raw will lend the best natural color to this cake.

MAKES ONE 9-INCH LOAF; COOK TIME: 60–65 MINUTES

FOR THE CAKE:

Pistachios, shelled	2.125 oz / ½ cup, plus 2 TB chopped pistachios for garnish
Butter, soft	10 oz / ½ cup plus 2 TB
White sugar	7 oz / 1 cup
Vanilla extract	2 tsp
Eggs	5 large
Brown rice flour	3.6 oz / ⅔ cup
Millet flour	2.5 oz / ½ cup
Tapioca starch	3 oz / ⅓ cup
Kosher salt	½ tsp
Xanthan gum	¾ tsp
Baking powder	1 tsp
Whole milk	4 oz / ½ cup

FOR THE WHITE GLAZE:

Powdered sugar	4 oz / 1 cup
Water	1.5 oz / 2 TB

1 Preheat the oven to 350°F. In the bowl of a food processor, grind ½ cup pistachios to a fine powder; it should resemble the texture of cornmeal. Take care not to overmix or you will wind up with pistachio paste.

2 In the bowl of a stand mixer fitted with the paddle attachment, cream together butter and sugar on high speed until light and fluffy, about 2 minutes. Using a spatula, scrape down the sides of the bowl to make sure all the butter and sugar is incorporated. Add vanilla and mix at medium speed very briefly to combine.

3 With the mixer running on low speed, add eggs, one at a time, waiting until each egg is fully incorporated before adding the next. Scrape down the sides of the bowl once or twice between additions. Continue to mix on medium speed for 2–3 minutes until eggs are fully incorporated into the mixture. It should look smooth and be a pale yellow color.

CONTINUED

4 Add brown rice flour, millet flour, tapioca starch, salt, xanthan gum, and baking powder to the bowl then add the finely ground pistachios and mix on low speed to combine. Scrape down the bottom and sides of the bowl, making sure to incorporate any bits of unmixed butter and sugar.

5 With the machine running on low, slowly pour in the milk. This should take 30 seconds or so. Once all the milk has been added, mix on high for 2 minutes until the batter is very light in color and fluffy.

6 Spray your loaf pan with cooking spray. Empty the batter into the pan, smoothing out the top and taking care to spread the mixture evenly to the sides. Cover with foil and bake for 45 minutes. Remove the foil and bake for an additional 15–20 minutes, until the cake springs back when gently pushed with your finger and is a light-gold color around the edges.

7 While the cake is baking, make the white glaze: In the bowl of a stand mixer fitted with the whisk attachment, mix powdered sugar on low speed to break up any large clumps, about 20 seconds. Slowly add water, increasing speed gradually until the glaze is shiny and free of any lumps. It will appear thick and opaque when spread on the cooled cake.

8 Allow the cake to cool for about 30 minutes in the pan, then unmold it onto a baking sheet or cooling rack set on a parchment-lined baking sheet to cool completely.

9 Once the cake is fully cooled, cut it into 8 slices but keep the slices together as a loaf. Once you've iced the cake, it's difficult to make clean slices. Spread the white glaze all over the top of the cake and sprinkle with the reserved pistachios to decorate. Refrigerate the cake until the glaze is set, then use a sharp knife to break through the top layer of glaze and divide the cake into the individual portions for serving.

CHOCOLATE & VANILLA MARBLED POUND CAKE

The marbling on this cake gives it a charmingly old-fashioned feel, which I love. Make sure when you're swirling the batter that you use a skewer that reaches all the way to the bottom of the pan so you can blend all the chocolate and vanilla layers together. Don't miss the step of soaking the cake in the vanilla syrup after baking. It helps the cake stay moist for longer and reinforces all the flavors. For an extra-special treat, serve with cocoa nib–infused whipped cream (see page 20).

MAKES ONE 9-INCH LOAF; COOK TIME: 60–65 MINUTES

FOR THE VANILLA CAKE:

Butter, soft	8 oz / ½ cup
White sugar	6 oz / ¾ cup
Vanilla extract	2 tsp
Eggs	3 large
Brown rice flour	5.5 oz / 1 cup
Millet flour	1.25 oz / ¼ cup
Tapioca starch	1.25 oz / ¼ cup
Kosher salt	½ tsp
Xanthan gum	¾ tsp
Baking powder	1 tsp
Whole milk	2 oz / ¼ cup

FOR THE CHOCOLATE CAKE:

Butter, soft	8 oz / ½ cup
White sugar	6 oz / ¾ cup
Vanilla extract	1 tsp
Eggs	4 large
Brown rice flour	5.5 oz / 1 cup
Millet flour	1.25 oz / ¼ cup
Cocoa powder	1.6 oz / ¼ cup
Kosher salt	½ tsp
Xanthan gum	¾ tsp
Baking powder	1¼ tsp
Whole milk	3 oz / ⅓ cup

FOR THE VANILLA SYRUP:

Water	4 oz / ½ cup
White sugar	4 oz / ½ cup
Vanilla extract	1 TB

Cocoa Nib Cream (page 20), optional, for serving

1 Preheat the oven to 350°F.

2 Make the vanilla cake: In the bowl of a stand mixer fitted with the paddle attachment, cream together butter and sugar at high speed until light and fluffy, about 2 minutes. Using a spatula, scrape down the sides of the bowl. Add vanilla and mix at medium speed very briefly just to combine.

3 With the mixer running on low speed, add eggs, one at a time, waiting until each egg is fully incorporated before adding the next. Scrape down the sides of the bowl once or twice between additions. It should look smooth and be a pale yellow color.

4 Add brown rice flour, millet flour, tapioca starch, salt, xanthan gum, and baking powder to the bowl and mix on low speed to combine. Scrape down the bottom and sides of the bowl, making sure to incorporate any bits of unmixed butter and sugar.

5 With the machine running on low, slowly pour in the milk. Once all milk has been added, mix on high for 2 minutes until the mixture is very light in color and fluffy. Transfer the vanilla cake batter to another bowl while you make the chocolate cake. No need to wash out your mixing bowl between the vanilla and chocolate cake batters.

6 Make the chocolate cake: Using the ingredients for chocolate cake, repeat steps 1–5. Spray your loaf pan with cooking spray.

7 Once you have both batters made, fill a piping bag with the chocolate batter. Starting and ending with the vanilla batter, spread one third of the vanilla mixture into the bottom of the prepared pan. Pipe in half of the chocolate mixture, making a swirly helix pattern on top of the vanilla batter. Spread in another third of the vanilla batter. (Don't worry if you mix some of the chocolate batter below in with the vanilla batter.) Pipe in the remaining half of the chocolate mixture. End with the remaining third of the vanilla batter, spreading it evenly over the top.

8 Using a long skewer or very sharp knife, swirl the batters together in the pan, reaching all the way to the bottom and into the corners.

This will create a lovely swirled pattern in the finished cake. When the batters have been sufficiently swirled together, cover the pan with foil and bake for 45–50 minutes. Remove the foil and bake for another 10–15 minutes, until the cake springs back when gently pushed with your finger and is a light-gold color around the edges.

9 While the cake is baking, make the vanilla syrup: In a small saucepan or in the microwave, heat the water until simmering. Whisk in the sugar and vanilla until the sugar is dissolved. Set aside until the cake is baked.

10 When the cake is finished baking, allow it to cool for 10 minutes in the pan then prick it all over the top with a fork. Pour the vanilla syrup over the surface of the cake, allowing it to soak the top and run down the sides, between the cake and the pan.

11 Allow the cake to cool for about 30 minutes in the pan, then unmold it onto a baking sheet or cooling rack to cool completely.

COCOA NIB CREAM

This easy method for making infused whipped cream is from one of my favorite baking books, Alice Medrich's *Bittersweet*. It's a genius technique that you can apply to any number of ingredients. I've used it to infuse cream with Earl Grey tea, coffee beans, and star anise, all with great results. All you need is cream, mix-ins, and 8 hours for the infusion to rest in the fridge before you whip and serve it the next day. Use the exact same procedure and timing for all of these ingredients. While all of these version are delicious, the cocoa nib cream still remains my favorite!

MAKES ABOUT 2 CUPS

Cocoa nibs	1.4 oz / ¼ cup
Heavy whipping cream	8 oz / 1 cup

1 Place the cocoa nibs and cream in a small bowl, cover with plastic wrap, and set aside overnight in the fridge to infuse.

2 When you're ready to serve, strain out the cocoa nibs and discard them. Whip the cream in a stand mixer fitted with the whisk attachment until soft peaks form. The cream remains a soft white when whipped yet tastes deliciously like chocolate!

PUMPKIN WALNUT BREAD WITH CREAM CHEESE ICING

We make this pumpkin bread every fall in the cafés and I look forward to it with great anticipation! I love fall flavors, and this recipe has all of those warm spices, plus crunchy nuts and my absolute-favorite cream cheese icing. This recipe is flexible as well. If walnuts aren't your thing, substitute toasted pecans, chocolate chips, or chopped candied ginger instead. All would be wonderful additions to the pumpkin and spices.

MAKES ONE 9-INCH LOAF; COOK TIME: 55–65 MINUTES

Butter, soft	3 oz / 7 TB
Vegetable oil	3 oz / ⅓ cup
White sugar	5.25 oz / ⅔ cup
Brown sugar	3.75 oz / ½ cup
Eggs	3 large
Vanilla extract	½ tsp
Pure pumpkin puree	1 (15-oz) can / 1½ cups
White rice flour	6.2 oz / 1¼ cups
Sorghum flour	2.25 oz / ½ cup
Baking soda	¾ tsp
Baking powder	1½ tsp
Xanthan gum	¾ tsp
Ground cinnamon	½ tsp
Ground nutmeg	½ tsp, plus more for garnish
Ground cardamom	½ tsp
Kosher salt	½ tsp
Raw walnuts, chopped	3.75 oz / ¾ cup
Vanilla Bean Cream Cheese Icing (page 113)	½ cup

1 Preheat the oven to 350°F. In the bowl of a stand mixer fitted with the paddle attachment, cream together butter, vegetable oil, and both sugars at medium speed until light and fluffy, about 2 minutes. Add eggs and vanilla and continue mixing until combined. Scrape down the sides of the bowl. Add pumpkin puree and mix until smooth.

2 Add white rice flour, sorghum flour, baking soda, baking powder, xanthan gum, cinnamon, nutmeg, cardamom, and salt to the bowl and mix at low speed to combine. Stir in walnuts and continue mixing until evenly incorporated, about 30 seconds. Scrape down the sides of the bowl, making sure all the butter and sugar is evenly combined.

CONTINUED

3 Spray a loaf pan with baking spray. Using a spatula, spread the batter evenly into the pan, pushing gently into the corners and leveling the top. Cover with foil and bake for 45–50 minutes. Remove the foil and bake until the top is an earthy medium brown and springs back when pressed gently with your finger, about 10–15 minutes longer. The cake will appear darker when fully baked as the pumpkin and spices in the batter lend a naturally darker color to the finished cake. Not to worry, it will be soft and moist on the inside.

4 Cool in the pan for 30 minutes, then invert onto a baking sheet or cooling rack to cool completely. This cake can be delicate when warm so make sure you allow it to fully cool before icing it. Cover the top with cream cheese icing and sprinkle with ground nutmeg to finish. Chill until firm enough to slice with a serrated knife, about 2 hours or overnight.

MORNING BAKED GOODS

Raspberry & Almond Scones

Cacao Nib & Walnut Coffee Cake

Vegan Lemon & Poppy Seed Muffins

Vegan Banana Muffins with Chocolate Chips

Luscious Iced Cinnamon Rolls

Lemon & Blueberry Coffee Cake

Vegan Baked Donuts

Sourdough Waffles

RASPBERRY & ALMOND SCONES

Hands down our best-selling item at the bakeshops from day one, these delicious scones are buttery, flaky, and perfect for any time of day. Nothing is better with a morning cup of coffee or an afternoon tea. The recipe makes a big batch, so keep any unbaked dough in your freezer to bake up for last-minute gatherings or a special weekend breakfast for the family.

MAKES 24 SCONES; COOK TIME: 22–28 MINUTES

Sweet scone dough (page 220, through Step 3), at room temperature	1 recipe
Almond extract	1 tsp
Sliced almonds	1½ oz / ½ cup, plus 2 TB for baking
Frozen raspberries (unthawed)	6.6 oz / 1½ cups
Heavy cream	2 TB, or more to taste
Brown rice flour, as needed for shaping	
Coarse sugar or crystal sugar	2 TB for baking

1 Put the sweet scone dough in the bowl of a stand mixer with the paddle attachment. Add almond extract, sliced almonds, and frozen raspberries. With the mixer on lowest speed, mix very briefly, just to combine. You want the raspberries to remain intact. If you overmix the dough, the raspberries will be broken and the dough will be pink.

2 Divide the dough into three equal-sized rounds and wrap each tightly in plastic wrap. Refrigerate for at least 30 minutes or overnight.

3 To shape the scones, flour your counter or cutting board with a light dusting of brown rice flour. Remove one round of chilled dough from the fridge at a time. Using floured hands, pat the dough into an 8-inch round, roughly 1 inch thick. Using a sharp knife or a floured bench scraper, shape the scones: Cut the dough round crosswise in half, then cut each half crosswise in half (you now have 4 pieces); cut each quarter in half yet again, forming 8 wedges. Repeat with the remaining 2 dough rounds to shape 24 scones in all.

4 Preheat the oven to 375°F. Place the scones on two parchment-lined baking sheets, spaced about 2 inches apart. Brush the scones with the heavy cream to your taste, sprinkle each scone with a few sliced almonds, and dust each one with a sprinkling of coarse sugar.

5 Bake the scones for 18 minutes in the middle half of the oven. Rotate the pans between upper and lower oven racks, and bake for another 8–10 minutes, until scones are lightly brown on the top and feel just set to the touch. Allow to cool for 10 minutes on the baking sheet before removing to a platter. Serve immediately with butter and jam.

CACAO NIB & WALNUT COFFEE CAKE

Not too sweet, with tons of great texture, including a crunchy, nutty top, a rich, buttery cake, and a dreamy cream-cheese surprise inside, this recipe is one you'll return to time and again. It manages to be both homey and impressive at the same time and continues to be a favorite both at our family table and with our customers. This keeps well at room temperature when made a day ahead and is the perfect treat for a holiday breakfast with family or a lazy Sunday brunch.

SERVES 10–12; COOK TIME: 45–50 MINUTES

FOR THE CAKE BATTER:

Butter, soft	6 oz / 1½ sticks
White sugar	3.5 oz / ½ cup
Brown sugar	3.75 oz / ½ cup
Eggs	2 large
Vanilla extract	1 tsp
Brown rice flour	6.875 oz / 1¼ cups
Millet flour	2.5 oz / ½ cup
Tapioca starch	1.125 oz / ¼ cup
Baking powder	1½ tsp
Baking soda	1 tsp
Kosher salt	½ tsp
Sour cream	8 oz / 1 cup

FOR THE FILLING:

Butter, soft	1 TB
Cream cheese, soft	8 oz / 1 package
White sugar	3.5 oz / ½ cup
Grand Marnier	1 TB
Cake batter (recipe above)	¾ cup

FOR THE CRUMBLE:

Chopped raw walnuts	4 oz / 1 cup
Cacao nibs	1.86 oz / ⅓ cup
Brown sugar	1.375 oz / ¼ cup
Butter, soft	2 TB
Ground cinnamon	½ tsp
Ground nutmeg	¼ tsp
Kosher salt	½ tsp

1 Preheat the oven to 350°F.

2 Make the cake batter: In the bowl of a stand mixer fitted with the paddle attachment, cream together the soft butter and both sugars on medium speed until the mixture is light and fluffy and pale in color, about 2 minutes. Scrape down the sides of the bowl to release any unmixed bits of butter and sugar. Add eggs and vanilla and mix to combine. Scrape down the bowl. Add brown rice flour, millet flour, tapioca starch, baking powder, baking soda, and salt, and mix on medium speed for 3–4 minutes until well incorporated. Add the sour cream and mix on medium speed for 2–3 minutes to combine. The sour cream will help to lighten the batter overall. Transfer batter to a small bowl and set aside.

3 Make the filling: In a stand mixer fitted with the same paddle attachment, combine the softened butter, cream cheese, and sugar in the same bowl used to mix the cake batter. Mix on high speed until smooth and no lumps remain. Add Grand Marnier and mix to combine. Add ¾ cup of the cake batter and mix to combine. Set aside.

4 Make the crumble: In the bowl of a food processor, combine all of the crumble ingredients. Process until a coarse crumb forms. You still want to see recognizable pieces of each ingredient but they should be held together in large crumble-like pieces.

5 Preheat the oven to 350°F. Spray a 10-cup bundt pan with baking spray. Scatter half of the crumble around the bottom of the pan. Add one third of the cake batter on top of the crumble. Smooth with a small offset spatula into an even layer. Dollop cream cheese filling on top of the cake batter. Smooth again with a small offset spatula to form a thick, even layer, covering the whole width of the pan, from center to edge. Add the remaining two thirds of the cake batter and smooth to cover all of the cream cheese filling. Scatter the remaining half of the crumble over the top.

6 Cover the cake with foil and bake at for 25 minutes. Remove foil and reduce the oven temperature to 325°F. Bake for another 20 minutes or until the top is a medium brown and feels just set and springy to the touch. The center of the cake, where the cream cheese layer is, will feel softer than the sides of the cake but should still feel set. Cool completely in the pan before unmolding and serving.

CACAO NIB & WALNUT COFFEE CAKE

VEGAN LEMON & POPPY SEED MUFFINS

I developed this recipe because I wanted a simple breakfast muffin to grab while heading out the door, one that had all the bright citrus flavor I love with a good dose of fiber, protein, and enough fuel to get me through a busy morning. The poppy seeds dotted throughout add a delicious crunch and a pleasing appearance, and the texture is light and springy, in part due to the applesauce that's used instead of dairy to keep the muffins moist. These are equally good in kids' lunchboxes, satisfying that need for a sweet snack in a healthier way.

MAKES 12–16 MUFFINS; COOK TIME: 20–25 MINUTES

Golden flaxseed meal	1 oz / 6 TB
Water	6 oz / ¾ cup
Applesauce	17.5 oz / 2 cups
Lemon juice	4 oz / ½ cup
Lemon zest	2 TB
Vanilla extract	1 tsp
Coconut oil, melted	3.7 oz / ½ cup
Unsweetened almond milk	4 oz / ½ cup
Light agave syrup	3 oz / ¼ cup
White sugar	5.25 oz / ¾ cup
Kosher salt	1 tsp
Baking soda	1 TB
Poppy seeds	2 TB
Gluten-free rolled oats	3.5 oz / 1 cup
Almond flour	3.38 oz / 1 cup
White rice flour	5 oz / 1 cup
Brown rice flour	2.75 oz / ½ cup
Tapioca starch	2.25 oz / ½ cup
Xanthan gum	2 tsp

1 Preheat the oven to 350°F.

2 Prepare flax "eggs": Soak flaxseed meal and water in a small bowl for 10–15 minutes until it forms a thick gel.

3 In the bowl of a stand mixer fitted with the paddle attachment, combine applesauce, lemon juice, lemon zest, vanilla, melted coconut oil, almond milk, agave syrup, sugar, and salt. Mix on low speed for 1–2 minutes to combine. When flax eggs are thick and gelled, add them to the wet ingredients and mix on medium speed for 2–3 minutes to combine.

4 Add baking soda and poppy seeds to the mixer bowl and mix on low speed for 1–2 minutes. The mixture will foam up dramatically. Don't worry! This is the baking soda reacting with the lemon juice. The foam will subside when you add the dry ingredients.

5 Add rolled oats, almond flour, white rice flour, brown rice flour, tapioca starch, and xanthum gum to the mixer and stir on low speed to combine.

6 Line 1–2 muffin tin(s) with paper muffin cups. Using a ⅓ cup cookie scoop, evenly divide the batter among the muffin cups, nearly filling them. You should get 12–16 muffins, depending on the size of your muffin cups.

7 Bake for 20–25 minutes, rotating the pan halfway through baking, until the muffins are evenly golden brown and spring back when touched gently with your finger. Let cool completely before removing from the pan. Muffins are best served at room temperature, which makes them the perfect treat to bring to a school or office party or for making the night before for a weekend brunch. When warm they can have a slightly sticky texture, so exercise patience and allow them to cool. As the muffins cool, they firm up and develop a pleasingly soft, springly texture. They are excellent with marmalade and/or almond butter.

VEGAN BANANA MUFFINS WITH CHOCOLATE CHIPS

Both vegan and gluten-free can be tricky to get just right, but these delectable muffins have a pleasingly moist and springy texture thanks to the addition of flax "eggs." Make a large batch on the weekend and pack them into school lunchboxes for a special treat or grab one for a quick breakfast on a busy weekday morning.

MAKES 18 MUFFINS; COOK TIME: 25–30 MINUTES

Golden flaxseed meal	3 TB
Water	⅔ cup
Ripe bananas, mashed	3 medium / 1 cup
Vegetable oil	4 oz / ½ cup
White sugar	7 oz / 1 cup
Vanilla extract	1 tsp
White rice flour	5.5 oz / 1 cup
Brown rice flour	2.75 oz / ½ cup
Tapioca starch	2.75 oz / ½ cup
Xanthan gum	1 tsp
Baking powder	2 tsp
Ground cinnamon	½ tsp
Kosher salt	½ tsp
Chocolate chips	4.5 oz / ¾ cup

1 Prepare flax "eggs": Soak flaxseed meal and water in a small bowl for 10–15 minutes until it forms a thick gel. Preheat the oven to 350°F.

2 In the bowl of a stand mixer fitted with the paddle attachment, combine mashed bananas, vegetable oil, sugar, and vanilla. Mix for 1–2 minutes on low speed until combined. When flax eggs are thick and gelled, add them to the wet ingredients and mix on low speed to combine. The mixture will be lumpy.

3 Add white rice flour, brown rice flour, tapioca starch, xanthan gum, baking powder, cinnamon, and salt to the mixer bowl and mix on low to combine. Add in chocolate chips and stir on low speed very briefly, just until evenly distributed.

4 Line 18 muffin cups with paper liners. Using a 2-ounce cookie scoop (#16, or about ¼ cup), scoop the batter into the prepared pan(s). Bake the muffins for 25–30 minutes until the tops are puffed and golden brown and spring back when gently pushed with your finger.

5 Cool the muffins for 5 minutes in the pan before unmolding them. Serve immediately or place them in zip-top bags and store in your freezer for up to one month. Defrost overnight at room temperature before serving.

LUSCIOUS ICED CINNAMON ROLLS

Who doesn't love a warm, gooey cinnamon roll?! When I became gluten-free, they were one of the baked goods I missed most. I went through dozens of trials and made lots of hard, dense rolls that didn't have that soft, pull-apart texture a good cinnamon roll should have. Two years and countless tests later, I finally felt this version was perfect enough for our daily bakery assortment. They have a crispy bottom, a doughy, pull-apart interior, and an assertive cinnamon kick in every bite. Our customers line up daily for these, enjoying them hot from the oven, which really is how they should be enjoyed. Be generous with the icing; it is delicious and equally good spread liberally on everything from pumpkin walnut bread (page 21) to scones (page 26).

MAKES 12–16 ROLLS; COOK TIME: 25–30 MINUTES

Whole milk	4 oz / ½ cup
Active dry yeast	1½ tsp
Butter	2 oz / ¼ cup
Brown sugar	7.5 oz / 1 cup
Ground cinnamon	1 oz / ¼ cup
White sugar	3.5 oz / ½ cup
Potato starch	3 oz / ½ cup
Brown rice flour	6.875 oz / 1¼ cups
Almond meal	2 oz / ½ cup
Tapioca starch	1.5 oz / ⅓ cup, plus more for rolling
Baking soda	½ tsp
Xanthan gum	1½ tsp
Baking powder	2 TB
Kosher salt	½ tsp
Butter, soft	2 TB
Eggs	2 large
Olive oil	1.75 oz / ¼ cup
Vanilla extract	½ tsp

FOR THE ICING:

Butter	4 oz / 1 stick
Cream cheese	4 oz / ½ package
Powdered sugar	6 oz / 1½ cups
Vanilla extract	1 tsp

1 In the microwave on high or on the stove-top over low heat, heat milk until lukewarm (about 105°F) and add yeast. Set aside to bloom for about 5 minutes.

2 Next, make the filling: In the microwave, melt the butter. Stir brown sugar and cinnamon into melted butter until combined. Set aside.

3 Make the dough: In the bowl of a stand mixer fitted with the paddle attachment, combine white sugar, potato starch, brown rice flour, almond meal, tapioca starch, baking soda, xanthan gum, baking powder, and salt. Mix together on low speed. Add the soft

CONTINUED

butter, eggs, olive oil, and vanilla to the bowl, along with the milk and bloomed yeast, and mix on high speed for 1½ minutes. The dough will be shiny and smooth.

4 On a work surface, spread out a large piece of plastic wrap, about 16 x 10 inches. Generously dust the plastic wrap with tapioca starch. Scoop big dollops of dough onto the plastic wrap, evenly spacing them down the length of the plastic. Dust your hands and a rolling pin with tapioca starch and roll the rolling pin over the dollops to create a single rectangle, measuring about 13 x 9 inches. If the dough sticks to your rolling pin, re-dust it with tapioca starch.

5 Using a small offset spatula, spread the brown sugar and cinnamon filling evenly over the rectangle of dough, leaving a 1-inch border on all sides. Use a pastry brush to remove any tapioca starch from the border then brush the border with water.

6 Using your plastic wrap to help you, and starting with the long side closest to you, roll up the dough lengthwise into a tight log. When you are done, the seam should face down.

7 Using a knife or a bench scraper dusted with tapioca starch, cut about 1 inch off each end of the roll, then cut your log crosswise in half. Cut each log crosswise in half again. You will now have 4 pieces. Slice each quarter into thirds or fourths to create 12 or 16 rolls, depending on your preference and the size of your baking dish.

8 Spray a 9 x 13-inch baking pan with nonstick spray. Carefully lift each roll and place it in the pan, cut side facing up. Place them closely together in the pan. It's fine if they're touching. Cover with plastic wrap and set aside to proof in a warm place for about 1 hour, until the rolls begin to rise. Then, set them aside in your refrigerator to proof for at least 4 hours or overnight.

9 When the dough is done proofing, preheat your oven to 350°F. Bake the cinnamon rolls, uncovered, for 25–30 minutes until evenly golden brown but still soft in the center.

10 While the cinnamon rolls are baking, make the icing: Soften the butter and cream cheese in the microwave for about 90 seconds. Scrape the softened butter and cream cheese into the bowl of a stand mixer fitted with the paddle attachment and mix together on high speed for about 2 minutes until no lumps remain. Add powdered sugar and mix until completely smooth. Mix in vanilla.

11 When the cinnamon rolls are finished baking, let cool for 5 minutes. Generously spread icing onto the warm cinnamon rolls and allow it to melt. Cool for another 5 minutes or so and then cut the rolls apart. When they're hot from the oven, the rolls may be too fragile to portion, so be patient and let them cool a bit before cutting them apart. These are best served warm on the same day they are baked. Or you can reheat them in the microwave for 20 seconds the next day to refresh the dough.

LEMON & BLUEBERRY COFFEE CAKE

I'm a big fan of the humble bundt cake. There's something so old-fashioned and homey, yet impressive, about its appearance. I collect vintage bundt pans and some of the designs are so intricate! Look for them at your local flea market or garage sales. A little scrub is all it takes to bring them back to life. I like this cake for so many reasons, most notably because it's ultra-light from the whipped eggs and sugar, which add so much airy goodness to the finished cake.

SERVES 10–12; COOK TIME: 40–45 MINUTES

Eggs	6 large
White sugar	10 oz / 1½ cups
Vanilla extract	1 TB
Lemon zest	1 TB
Brown rice flour	6.875 oz / 1¼ cups
Millet flour	2.5 oz / ½ cup
Tapioca starch	1.125 oz / ¼ cup
Baking powder	1 TB
Xanthan gum	½ tsp
Kosher salt	1 tsp
Butter, melted	4 oz / 1 stick
Vegetable oil	3.5 oz / ½ cup
Blueberries, fresh or frozen (not thawed)	5.2 oz / 1 cup

1 In the bowl of a stand mixer fitted with the whisk attachment, whip eggs, sugar, vanilla, and lemon zest on high speed for 3–5 minutes, until the mixture has doubled in volume and thick ribbons fall off the end of the whisk when lifted.

2 Add brown rice flour, millet flour, tapioca starch, baking powder, xanthan gum, and salt and mix on low speed until just combined.

3 Slowly add the melted butter and vegetable oil, mixing on medium speed until well combined, about 2 minutes.

4 Cover the bowl with plastic wrap and refrigerate for about 20 minutes to allow the proteins to rest and the batter to thicken.

5 Preheat the oven to 325°F. Thoroughly spray a 10-cup bundt pan with nonstick spray.

6 After the batter has rested, gently fold in the blueberries, taking care not to overmix or the batter will be streaky.

7 Pour the batter into the prepared pan. Bake for 40–45 minutes, rotating the pan halfway through baking, until the cake is golden brown and springs back when touched. Let cool in the pan at least 30 minutes before unmolding. The cake will keep tightly wrapped in plastic wrap in the refrigerator for up to 5 days.

VEGAN BAKED DONUTS

These tender, cake-style donuts are perfect for a special weekend treat, classroom party, or wedding dessert table, and are beloved by kids of all ages. At our bakeshops, we make dozens of these daily, and the flavors are endlessly adaptable. I've included a handful of variations below but feel free to use your imagination! The simple glaze comes together in a snap and is equally adaptable to different flavor variations. Even without a glaze, a simple dusting of cinnamon sugar makes these special.

MAKES 12 DONUTS; COOK TIME: ABOUT 10 MINUTES

Brown rice flour	4.125 oz / ¾ cup
Millet flour	1.25 oz / ¼ cup
Tapioca starch	1.125 oz / ¼ cup
Potato starch	3 oz / ½ cup
White sugar	7 oz / 1 cup
Baking powder	1½ tsp
Baking soda	⅛ tsp
Kosher salt	½ tsp
Xanthan gum	½ tsp
Ground cinnamon	1 tsp
Ground cardamom	½ tsp
Ground nutmeg	½ tsp
Unsweetened applesauce	4.375 oz / ½ cup
Hot water	4 oz / ½ cup
Vegetable oil	2.33 oz / ⅓ cup
Vanilla extract	2 tsp

VANILLA GLAZE:

Powdered sugar	8.8 oz / 2 cups
Hot water	2 oz / 4 TB
Vanilla extract	1 tsp

1 Preheat the oven to 400°F. In the bowl of a stand mixer fitted with the paddle attachment, combine brown rice flour, millet flour, tapioca starch, potato starch, white sugar, baking powder, baking soda, salt, xanthan gum, cinnamon, cardamom, and nutmeg. Mix on low speed just until combined.

2 Slowly add applesauce, hot water, vegetable oil, and vanilla to the dry ingredients and mix on low speed until the batter is smooth, about 2 minutes.

3 Spray two 6-compartment donut pans with nonstick spray. Pipe or spoon the batter into the pans, dividing it equally among the 12 compartments and filling each about three-fourths full. Bake for 10 minutes until the donuts are golden brown and just set. Cool in the pans for 10 minutes before unmolding the donuts on a wire rack.

4 Make the vanilla glaze: In a shallow bowl, whisk together the powdered sugar, hot water, and vanilla. Dip the donuts into the bowl to coat, letting the excess glaze drip off. Return them to the wire rack to let the glaze set.

CONTINUED

VARIATIONS: DONUTS

Chocolate: Substitute ¼ cup cocoa powder for the potato starch. Omit the spices or use cardamom and/or cinnamon. Finish with a chocolate glaze (see recipe).

Pumpkin Spice: Substitute pumpkin puree for the applesauce and increase the hot water to 6 tablespoons. Finish with a maple glaze (see recipe).

Banana Walnut: Substitue 1 mashed, ripe banana for the applesauce. Add ¼ cup chopped walnuts to the batter. Finish with chocolate or maple glaze (see recipes).

Lemon Poppy Seed: Add 1 tablespoon lemon zest and 1 tablespoon poppy seeds to the batter and omit the spices. Finish with a lemon glaze (see recipe).

Chocolate Espresso: Substitute ¼ cup cocoa powder for the potato starch. Omit the spices. Swap ¼ cup brewed or instant espresso for the hot water. Finish with a coffee glaze (see recipe).

VARIATIONS: GLAZE

Chocolate: Replace the powdered sugar with ¼ cup cocoa powder.

Maple: Replace 2 tablespoons of the hot water with maple syrup.

Coffee: Replace 2 tablespoons of the hot water with brewed espresso.

Lemon: Replace 2 tablespoons of the hot water with fresh lemon juice.

SOURDOUGH WAFFLES

Included in the Master Recipe chapter is my formula for a gluten-free sourdough starter. Anyone who keeps and feeds a starter is always looking for a new way to use it, and I can pretty much guarantee that these crispy, light, and extra-delicious waffles are reason enough to nurture your starter regularly. Make sure you plan ahead for this recipe as it requires that you mix a simple sponge the night before you actually cook the waffles. The extra overnight fermentation lends excellent flavor to the waffles, and it takes just a minute to mix it up the evening before.

These waffles are equally good made sweet or savory. When I'm in need of a quick dinner, I reheat them straight from the freezer on a baking sheet in a preheated 350°F oven for 10–15 minutes until re-crisped. Then I serve them with any number of toppings I have on hand like poached eggs, leftover roasted vegetables or pesto, smoked salmon, or fresh herbs.

MAKES 4 WAFFLES; COOK TIME: ABOUT 10 MINUTES

FOR THE OVERNIGHT SPONGE:

Sourdough starter, unfed (page 209, Step 2 to bubbles forming)	8 oz / 1 cup
Buttermilk	8.5 oz / 1 cup
White rice flour	2.5 oz / ½ cup
Sorghum flour	2.75 oz / ½ cup
Brown sugar	1 TB

FOR THE BATTER:

Eggs	1 large
Butter, melted	2 oz / ¼ cup
Vanilla extract	½ tsp
Kosher salt	½ tsp
Baking soda	1 tsp
Xanthan gum	½ tsp

1 Put all the ingredients for the overnight sponge in a large bowl and whisk to combine. Cover with plastic wrap and allow to rest at least 8 hours or overnight at room temperature.

2 The next morning, or after 8 hours, whisk all the ingredients for the waffle batter into the sponge.

3 Preheat the waffle iron. Spray the iron with nonstick spray. Ladle about ½ cup batter into the waffle maker and cook until golden brown and crispy. Repeat with the remaining batter. Serve immediately or freeze, stored in zip-top bags, for up to 3 months. Reheat the waffles in a preheated 350°F oven for 10 minutes and they're honestly as good as the day they were made!

CONTINUED

Note: You won't regret making a double batch on the weekend and keeping them on hand in the freezer. They're equally good topped with maple syrup and berries as they are with soft poached eggs, greens, and crème fraîche, if you prefer a savory version.

VARIATION:

Sourdough Pancakes: Heat a pancake griddle or large nonstick skillet over medium heat. Add 1 tablespoon butter and swirl to coat the pan. Ladle in batter for pancakes of whatever size you prefer. Flip when the pancakes just begin to bubble at the edges and cook until golden brown, about 2 minutes per side. Repeat with remaining batter. Serve immediately with your favorite sweet or savory toppings.

MAKE-AHEAD BREAKFASTS

Baked Oatmeal with Berries

Bircher with Dried Fruit & Nuts

Chocolatey Chia Pudding

Coziest Breakfast Porridge

Savory Scones with Roasted Pears,
Blue Cheese & Walnuts

Triple-Ginger Buttermilk Biscuits

BAKED OATMEAL WITH BERRIES

Hands-down, this is my husband Rick's favorite breakfast. He loves it so much he has been eating it literally every day for years! I make a large pan on Sunday and he portions it out every morning and reheats in the microwave before work. After drizzling it with a little almond milk or a dollop of yogurt, he's fueled with a hot meal and ready to greet the day ahead. Feel free to use whatever fresh or frozen berries or cut fruit you have on hand.

SERVES 6; COOK TIME: 40–45 MINUTES

Gluten-free rolled oats	7 oz / 2 cups
Brown sugar	3.75 oz / ½ cup
Whole raw almonds	3.75 oz / ¾ cup
Raw walnuts, halves and pieces	3 oz / ¾ cup
Ground cinnamon	1 tsp
Ground cardamom	½ tsp
Kosher salt	½ tsp
Vanilla paste	1 tsp
Coconut or almond milk	1½ cups
Egg	1 large
Mixed berries, fresh or frozen	7.5 oz / 1½ cups

1 Preheat the oven to 375°F. Mix all ingredients, except berries, together in a large bowl.

2 Spread berries in the bottom of a 9 x 13-inch baking dish. Using a spatula, spread the oatmeal mixture evenly over the top of the berries, flattening it just slightly.

3 Bake for 40–45 minutes, until the top is golden brown and crunchy and berries are bubbling. When the oatmeal has cooled to room temperature, cover with plastic and refrigerate until ready to serve.

BIRCHER WITH DRIED FRUITS & NUTS

Bircher is the European version of our overnight oats. Whatever you call it, it's a filling, healthy, fiber-rich way to start your day. It's easily made vegan by substituting the yogurt for coconut yogurt, or more coconut milk. One batch makes enough for the whole week so make it on Sunday, put in the fridge overnight, and you have breakfast ready to go for the week ahead.

MAKES ABOUT 8 CUPS

Gluten-free rolled oats	7 oz / 2 cups
Raw almonds, whole	3.75 oz / ¾ cup
Raw walnuts, chopped	3 oz / ¾ cup
Brown sugar or coconut sugar	2.5 oz / ⅓ cup
Kosher salt	1 tsp
Ground cinnamon	1 tsp
Unsweetened applesauce	8.75 oz / 1 cup
Light coconut milk	15 oz / 1½ cups
Plain yogurt (or kefir)	4 oz / ½ cup, plus more for topping, optional
Vanilla paste (or extract)	1 tsp
Dried blueberries (or cherries)	2 oz / ½ cup, plus more for topping, optional
Almond milk and granola	for topping (optional)

1 In a large bowl, mix together the oats, nuts, sugar, salt, and cinnamon.

2 Add the remaining ingredients all at once to the bowl. Stir to combine.

3 Place in a food storage container with a tight-fitting lid. Let the mixture rest overnight in the refrigerator. The oats will absorb the liquid and the mixture will thicken up the longer it sits.

4 To serve, top the chilled bircher with more yogurt (or kefir) and berries or with almond milk and granola.

CHOCOLATEY CHIA PUDDING

This is part breakfast and part dessert. I've enjoyed it for both purposes! It's just a tad sweet, super chocolatey, and will give you enough sustained energy to keep you happily full until lunch. It's also vegan but is so rich and creamy you'd never know. My favorite all-day way to serve this is topped with fresh berries and crunchy cacao nibs. I'll fully admit to eating this in lieu of dinner once or twice, drizzled with freshly brewed espresso, brandied cherries, and topped with whipped coconut cream. Any way you choose to eat it, you can't go wrong! Though this recipe requires no actual cooking, it does require you to mix it the evening before you wish to serve, so be sure to plan ahead.

MAKES ABOUT 6 CUPS

Chia seeds	2.8 oz / ½ cup
Cocoa powder	1 oz / ⅓ cup
Maple syrup	2 oz / ¼ cup
Ground cinnamon	1 tsp
Kosher salt	½ tsp
Vanilla paste (or extract)	1 tsp
Whole coconut milk	30 oz / 3 cups

1 In a large bowl, whisk together all ingredients until combined.

2 Refrigerate overnight in individual jars or a large food storage container with a tight-fitting lid before eating. The chia seeds will absorb all the liquid and form a thick, pudding-like mixture.

3 The pudding will keep well for up to 5 days. Enjoy chilled.

COZIEST BREAKFAST PORRIDGE

There is nothing better on a chilly morning than a bowl of steaming hot porridge. The best thing about porridge in my opinion is that you can substitute any type of cereal you like (quinoa, amaranth, millet, polenta, etc.) and apply the same technique. Porridge is also a sturdy blank canvas for all your favorite toppings. For breakfast, I especially enjoy mine with homemade applesauce, almond butter, and granola.

MAKES ABOUT 4 CUPS; COOK TIME: ABOUT 20 MINUTES

Water	32 oz / 4 cups
Gluten-free steel cut oats	6 oz / 1 cup
Kosher salt	1 tsp
Light coconut milk	10 oz / 1 cup
Brown sugar or coconut sugar (optional)	1.75 oz / ¼ cup

1 Bring the water to a boil in a medium saucepan over high heat. Whisk in the oats in a steady stream. Stir in the salt. Bring the mixture to a boil then reduce the heat to low and simmer, stirring occasionally, for about 20 minutes until thick and creamy.

2 Stir in the coconut milk. Stir in the sugar (if using). Serve warm with the toppings of your choice. This porridge can also be made well ahead and served later. You may need to add a touch more coconut milk (or water) when reheating if it has firmed up in the fridge.

SAVORY SCONES WITH ROASTED PEARS, BLUE CHEESE & TOASTED WALNUTS

In my opinion, savory scones are one of the best breakfast treats around. You get the satisfaction of a buttery morning pastry but aren't left feeling over-sugared when you're finished. I love the classic combination of pears, walnuts, and blue cheese as the scones are a little sweet from the pears, super savory from the blue cheese, and contain lots of crunchy bits from the walnuts. But the variations on this are many. A few of our customer favorites at the bakery are cheddar and chives; goat cheese and sundried tomatoes; and Gruyère, apple, and rosemary.

MAKES 24 SCONES; COOK TIME: 25–30 MINUTES FOR SCONES, PLUS 25–30 MINUTES FOR ROASTING PEARS

Pears, chopped into 1-inch cubes	10 oz / 2 cups, from about 2 large pears
Brown sugar	1.75 oz / ¼ cup
Ground cardamom	1 tsp
Ground cinnamon	1 tsp
Kosher salt	½ tsp
Raw walnuts	4 oz / 1 cup, plus 2 TB for baking
Savory Scones dough (page 222, through Step 3), at room temperature	1 recipe
Blue cheese, crumbled	3.5 oz / ¾ cup
Brown rice flour, for rolling	
Heavy cream	2 TB
Coarse sea salt	1 TB, for baking

1 Preheat the oven to 375°F. Line two baking sheets with parchment. On the first pan, toss together the pears, brown sugar, cardamom, cinnamon, and kosher salt. Roast until the pears are tender, 25–30 minutes. Meanwhile, spread out the walnuts on the second baking sheet in a single layer. After the pears have roasted for about 20 minutes, put the nuts in the oven on another rack and roast until light golden and fragrant, about 10 minutes. Place both baking sheets on wire racks and let the pears and walnuts cool slightly before proceeding with the recipe.

2 Put the savory scone dough in a bowl, add the roasted pears, blue cheese, and toasted walnuts. Stir together, just to combine. You want the mix-ins to remain intact.

3 Divide the dough evenly into three pieces, shape into balls, and wrap each one tightly in plastic wrap. Refrigerate for at least 30 minutes or up to overnight.

CONTINUED

4 To shape the scones, flour your counter or cutting board with a light dusting of brown rice flour. Using floured hands, pat the chilled dough into three 8-inch rounds, roughly 1 inch thick. Using a sharp knife or a floured bench scraper, cut one of the dough rounds crosswise in half, then cut each half crosswise in half (you now have 4 pieces); cut each quarter in half yet again, forming 8 wedges. Repeat with the other 2 rounds of dough to create 24 scones in all.

5 Preheat the oven to 375°F. Place the scones on two parchment-lined baking sheets, spaced about 2 inches apart. Brush the scones with heavy cream and sprinkle each one with a little coarse salt and a few of the reserved walnuts.

6 Bake for 25–30 minutes, rotating the pan halfway through baking, until the scones are lightly brown on the top and feel just set to the touch. Allow to cool for 10 minutes on the baking sheet before removing them as hot scones can be fragile and prone to breakage.

TRIPLE-GINGER BUTTERMILK BISCUITS

Biscuits are such a great staple for your baking toolbox as they carefully walk the line between sweet and savory. This version is tangy from the buttermilk and a little sweet from the candied ginger, and equally great served with Creamy Butternut Squash Soup (page 202) or simply with butter and apricot jam.

MAKES 24 BISCUITS; COOK TIME: 20–25 MINUTES

White rice flour	15 oz / 3 cups, plus more for rolling
Sorghum flour	13.5 oz / 3 cups
White sugar	5.25 oz / ¾ cup
Baking powder	4 TB
Kosher salt	2 tsp
Xanthan gum	2 tsp
Ground ginger	1 TB
Butter, cold	12 oz / 3 sticks
Eggs	4 large
Buttermilk	20 oz / 2½ cups, plus 2 TB for baking
Fresh ginger, grated	2 TB
Candied ginger, chopped	½ cup
Coarse or crystal sugar	2 TB, for baking

1 In the bowl of a stand mixer fitted with the paddle attachment, mix together the white rice flour, sorghum flour, sugar, baking powder, salt, xanthan gum, and ground ginger at medium speed until combined.

2 Cut the cold butter into 1-inch pieces. Add butter to dry ingredients and mix on low speed until the butter is incorporated and the mixture resembles coarse meal, about 2 minutes. The pieces of butter should be the size of peas.

3 Add all the eggs at once and mix at medium speed until just incorporated. Add the buttermilk and the fresh and candied ginger and mix on low speed until the dough is smooth, 1–2 minutes.

4 Divide the dough into three equal-sized rounds and wrap each tightly in plastic wrap. Refrigerate at least 30 minutes, or up to overnight.

5 Preheat the oven to 350°F. To shape the biscuits, you will need a 3-inch round biscuit cutter. Flour your counter or cutting board with a light dusting of rice flour. Using floured hands or a rolling pin, pat or roll out each piece of dough into a 10-inch round, roughly 1 inch thick. Using your biscuit cutter, punch out 8 disks from each round. Gather any dough scraps and re-roll them just once—if you re-roll more than once the biscuits will have picked up too much of the bench flour and will be dry and won't rise properly.

6 Place the biscuits on two parchment-lined baking sheets, spaced about 2 inches apart. Brush them with the reserved 2 tablespoons buttermilk, and sprinkle them with a light dusting of coarse sugar.

7 Bake for 15 minutes. Rotate pans and bake another 5–8 minutes until biscuits are barely golden on top and feel just set to the touch. Allow to cool for 5 minutes on the baking sheet before removing. Serve with butter and jam or freeze in zip-top bags for up to 1 month. To reheat, just refresh in a 350°F oven for 5–7 minutes before serving.

COOKIES

Triple-Chocolate Flourless Cookies

Salted Butter Chocolate Chip Cookies

Ginger-Molasses Whoopie Pies

Honey Shortbread Rollouts

Vegan Oatmeal Raisin Cookies

TRIPLE-CHOCOLATE FLOURLESS COOKIES

These cookies are for those of us, me included, who really, really love chocolate. They're ultrarich, fudgy, and decadent in every way. I use a bittersweet chocolate (70 percent cacao) here as I prefer a darker, more bitter flavor. If you prefer a sweeter flavor, try using a semisweet chocolate (54–60 percent cacao). Since the chocolate is really the star of the show, the quality you use will make a big difference in flavor. Use Valrhona chocolate if you can find it but Guittard and Scharffen Berger are also great, and readily available at most well-stocked supermarkets.

MAKES 24 COOKIES; COOK TIME: ABOUT 12 MINUTES

Butter	4 oz / 1 stick
Bittersweet chocolate, chopped	27 oz / 4½ cups
Eggs	6 large
Brown sugar	15 oz / 2 cups
Cocoa powder	2.25 oz / ¾ cup
Chocolate chips	6 oz / 1 cup

1 Preheat the oven to 350°F. Line two baking sheets with parchment paper. Melt the butter and chopped chocolate together in the microwave or over a double boiler. Stir every 45 seconds or so, taking care not to burn the chocolate. Whisk the melted butter and chocolate to combine.

2 Meanwhile, in the bowl of a stand mixer fitted with the whisk attachment, whip together the eggs, brown sugar, and cocoa powder until tripled in volume, 5–7 minutes.

3 Pour the whipped sugar and egg mixture into a large mixing bowl. Add the melted butter and chocolate and gently fold the two

mixtures together, taking care not to deflate the egg mixture. When the mixtures are evenly combined, gently stir in the chocolate chips.

4 Using a 2-ounce cookie scoop (#16, or about ¼ cup), scoop the batter onto the prepared baking sheets, leaving 2 inches of space between the cookies. You will fit about 8 cookies per sheet. These cookies spread a lot during baking! Depending on the size of your oven and how many baking sheets you have, you may need to work in batches.

5 Bake for 8 minutes, rotate the sheets between upper and lower oven racks, and bake for another 4 minutes, until the edges are just barely set and the middle still feels quite mushy. Take care not to overbake. You want these fudgy and soft. They will firm up as they cool. When a baking sheet has cooled, continue with the remaining dough. Store at room temperature for up to 2 days or in the freezer in a zip-top bag up to 1 month.

SALTED BUTTER CHOCOLATE CHIP COOKIES

Equally loved by both children and adults, this cookie is a classic. The saltiness balances the sweetness nicely here and gives these treats a more refined character. Using both a salted butter and kosher salt in the actual cookie contributes two levels of flavor, more of a background saltiness from the butter and a forward saltiness from the kosher salt. Adding the salt in this way gives the finished cookies a well-seasoned, rounded flavor that makes it hard to eat just one. Use your favorite chocolate, bittersweet or semisweet.

MAKES 24 COOKIES; COOK TIME: ABOUT 15 MINUTES

Salted butter, soft	1 pound / 4 sticks
White sugar	14 oz / 2 cups
Brown sugar	7.5 oz / 1 cup
Eggs	4 large
Vanilla extract	2 tsp
Brown rice flour	22 oz / 4 cups
Kosher salt	1 TB
Xanthan gum	½ tsp
Baking soda	1 tsp
Chocolate chips	6 oz / 1½ cups

1 In a stand mixer fitted with the paddle attachment, cream together butter and both sugars on medium speed until light and fluffy, 3–4 minutes. Scrape down the sides of the bowl twice during creaming.

2 With the mixer running on low speed, add eggs, one at a time, and vanilla. Continue to mix batter on medium speed until smooth, about 3 minutes, scraping down the bowl as needed to incorporate.

3 Add brown rice flour, salt, xanthan gum, and baking soda. Mix dough at medium speed until smooth, making sure to scrape the bowl to incorporate bits of unmixed sugar lingering on the bottom. Add chocolate chips and mix on low speed until just incorporated.

4 Line 2 baking sheets with parchment paper. Using a 1.5-ounce cookie scoop (#24, or about 3 tablespoons), scoop out dough onto the prepared baking sheets, leaving 2 inches of space between cookies. Each cookie ball should be about 2 inches in diameter; you should be able to fit about 8 cookies on each sheet. Refrigerate for at least 30 minutes or up to overnight before baking. Chilling the dough will help control the spread of the cookies while baking. If your dough is too soft, the dough will spread out and the cookie will be thinner and crispier. Chilled dough will spread less during baking, maintaining a thicker, chewier cookie with an even shape.

5 Preheat the oven to 350°F. Bake for about 8 minutes, rotate the sheets between upper and lower racks, and bake for another 7 minutes, , until cookies are a light golden brown around the edges and still soft in the center. Cool on the baking sheet completely before transferring to a serving platter or enjoying; the warm cookies are very fragile and can break easily. Repeat with the remaining dough.

Make-ahead tips: Scoop the dough balls and place them very close together on a baking sheet; freeze overnight until very hard. Bake your desired cookie quantity per the instructions above, straight from the freezer, adding 1–2 extra minutes to the baking time. Place the rest of the frozen dough balls in a zip-top plastic bag and keep in your freezer until needed, up to 3 months.

SALTED BUTTER CHOCOLATE CHIP COOKIES

GINGER-MOLASSES
WHOOPIE PIES

GINGER-MOLASSES WHOOPIE PIES

These cookies are spicy, chewy, and not too sweet. The recipe suggests filling them with Flour Craft's favorite cream cheese icing, but they are equally great filled with vanilla ice cream to make creamy ice cream sandwiches for hot summer days. They're also great on their own, made smaller, and served like a gingersnap with hot cocoa, or even lemon sorbet. Or, use the dough as a crust for our Pumpkin Cheesecake Bars with Ginger Cookie Crust (page 82).

MAKES 12 SANDWICH COOKIES; COOK TIME: ABOUT 20 MINUTES

Butter, soft	8 oz / 2 sticks
White sugar	7 oz / 1 cup
Brown sugar	7.5 oz / 1 cup
Large eggs	2 each
Vanilla extract	1 TB
Molasses (not blackstrap)	3.6 oz / ⅓ cup
Freshly grated ginger	1½ TB
Brown rice flour	16.5 oz / 3 cups
Cocoa powder	1.5 oz / ½ cup
Baking powder	1½ tsp
Kosher salt	1 TB
Baking soda	1 tsp
Xanthan gum	½ tsp
Ground cinnamon	1 tsp
Ground ginger	2 tsp
Ground cardamom	1 tsp
Ground nutmeg	1 tsp
Vanilla Bean Cream Cheese Icing (page 113) or vanilla ice cream, softened (for filling)	2 cups

1 Preheat the oven to 350°F. Line two baking sheets with parchment.

2 In the bowl of a stand mixer fitted with the paddle attachment, cream together butter and both sugars on medium speed until light and fluffy, 3–4 minutes. Add eggs all at once and vanilla and mix until smooth, about 2 minutes more, scraping down the bowl once or twice during mixing. Add molasses and freshly grated ginger and mix 1–2 minutes to combine.

3 Add brown rice flour, cocoa powder, baking powder, salt, baking soda, xanthan gum, cinnamon, ginger, cardamom, and nutmeg. Mix on low speed until evenly incorporated, 2–3 minutes, scraping down the bowl once or twice during mixing.

4 Using a 1.5-ounce cookie scoop (#24, or about 3 tablespoons), scoop dough balls onto the prepared baking sheets, spacing them about 1 inch apart. You should be able to fit 12 cookies per sheet. Chill in the refrigerator for 1 hour before baking or freeze until ready to use.

5 Bake for 20 minutes total, rotating pans between upper and lower oven racks half-way through baking. Cookies should feel just set around the edges and still soft in the middle. They will firm up when they cool. You want a soft, chewy cookie for your sandwich cookies.

6 When the cookies are fully cooled, sandwich 2–2½ tablespoons cream cheese icing or softened ice cream between 2 cookies and repeat with the remaining cookies. Chill until ready to serve.

Make-ahead tips: Whoopie pies will keep in the refrigerator, well wrapped in plastic, for up to 5 days. Ice cream sandwiches will keep, individually wrapped in the freezer, for up to 1 month.

HONEY SHORTBREAD ROLLOUTS

These cookies are my version of the classic sugar cookie. They're buttery and sturdy, with hints of lemon zest, perfect for cutting out into festive shapes and baking with sprinkles, or decorating with any number of tasty glazes (page 42). We make hundreds of these at our shops for every holiday, which are quickly devoured by adults and kids alike.

MAKES ABOUT THIRTY 3-INCH COOKIES, DEPENDING ON SHAPE; COOK TIME: ABOUT 10 MINUTES

Butter, soft	12 oz / 3 sticks
White sugar	9.3 oz / 1⅓ cup
Honey	4.5 oz / ⅓ cup
Lemon zest	1 TB
Brown rice flour	20.6 oz / 3¾ cups, plus more for rolling
Tapioca starch	2.25 oz / ½ cup
Millet flour	2.5 oz / ½ cup
Kosher salt	1 tsp
Xanthan gum	½ tsp
Sour cream	4 oz / ½ cup
Colored sprinkles (optional, for decorating)	6 oz / ½ cup

1 In the bowl of a stand mixer fitted with the paddle attachment, cream together butter, sugar, honey, and lemon zest on medium speed until light and fluffy, about 3 minutes.

2 Add brown rice flour, tapioca starch, millet flour, salt, and xanthan gum to the mixer bowl. Mix on low speed to combine, about 2–3 minutes. Scrape down the sides of the bowl. Add sour cream and mix on low until sour cream is fully incorporated and mixture is light and fluffy, about 1 minute more. Dough will feel quite soft, somewhere between a cake batter and a cookie dough.

3 Line a baking sheet with parchment. Using a small offset spatula, spread the dough evenly onto the baking sheet into a 9 x 13-inch rectangle, about ½ inch thick. Chill for at least 30 minutes or up to overnight.

4 Preheat the oven to 325°F. Line two baking sheets with parchment. When the dough is chilled, dust your counter with a small amount of rice flour. Working in batches, cut the chilled dough into quarters and roll out one quarter of the dough at a time. Sprinkle a small amount of flour on your rolling pin and roll dough ¼ inch thick. Cut into whichever shapes you fancy and, using a spatula, lift cut-out shapes onto the lined baking sheets. Work quickly here and keep remaining dough chilled while you work; soft dough will be more difficult to work with than chilled dough.

5 Dust cut-out shapes with sprinkles (if using). Bake for about 10 minutes, depending on size of cutouts, rotating sheet pans between upper and lower oven racks halfway through baking to ensure they brown evenly. Cookies should be barely golden on the edges and just set. Cool on wire racks and continue baking and rolling in batches. If decorating with icing, wait until cookies are fully cooled. These cookies keep well for up to 2 weeks; store them at room temperature in an airtight container or zip-top bag. They are also perfect for gifting and look lovely when presented in a clear cellophane bag tied with a festive ribbon.

VEGAN OATMEAL RAISIN COOKIES

I have no willpower when it comes to these cookies! I love the butteriness that comes from the ground nuts and the pops of bursty currants and warm spices. The only sweetener is maple syrup and they're entirely vegan, so in my opinion they're practically a breakfast cookie.

MAKES 18 COOKIES; COOK TIME: ABOUT 20 MINUTES

Raw pecans or walnuts	18 oz / 4 cups
Gluten-free rolled oats	7 oz / 2 cups
Baking powder	1½ tsp
Kosher salt	1 tsp
Tapioca starch	1 TB
Xanthan gum	1 tsp
Ground cinnamon	1 tsp
Ground nutmeg	¼ tsp
Ground cardamom	½ tsp
Olive oil	3.5 oz / ½ cup
Maple syrup	5.5 oz / ½ cup
Vanilla extract	1 tsp
Currants	4 oz / 1 cup

1 Preheat the oven to 325°F. Line two baking sheets with parchment paper. In a food processor, grind nuts until very finely ground, 3–4 minutes. You are looking for the texture of almond flour, a fine meal. Take care not to blend too far or you will make nut butter.

2 In the bowl of a stand mixer fitted with the paddle attachment, put the ground nuts and the rolled oats, baking powder, salt, tapiocha starch, xanthan gum, cinnamon, nutmeg, and cardamom. Mix on low speed, just to combine, about 1 minute. Add olive oil, maple syrup, and vanilla and continue mixing, until ingredients are evenly moistened and the mixture starts to hold together, about 2 minutes more. Stir in currants on low speed until just combined.

3 Using a 1.5-ounce scoop (#24, or about 3 tablespoons), scoop dough balls onto the prepared baking sheets, leaving 2 inches of space between them. You will need to press the dough firmly into the cookie scoop, so it forms a tight ball when scooped onto a baking sheet. If the balls are not tight enough, the dough will not hold together when pressed in Step 4.

4 Bake cookies for 10 minutes. Remove baking sheets from the oven and using a piece of parchment paper or a large spatula, press cookie balls into flat disks. Return the pans to the oven and bake another 10 minutes until cookies are the lightest golden brown and feel set at the edge. They will firm and crisp up as they cool.

BARS

Vegan Fruit Crumble Bars

Vegan Tahini & Halvah Brownies

Super Lemony Lemon Bars

Pumpkin Cheesecake Bars with
Ginger Cookie Crust

Raspberry Cheesecake Bars with
Chocolate Shortbread Crust

Maple-Whiskey Pecan Pie Bars with
Shortbread Crust

VEGAN FRUIT CRUMBLE BARS

Jammy, crunchy, fruity—these fruit bars are just plain scrumptious. The key here is to wait until they're chilled to cut them into tidy bars. The coconut oil must fully chill to be firm enough to hold them together. Use whatever berries, fresh or frozen, you have on hand or what you like most. I've made these bars with freshly picked blackberries and with a bag of frozen mixed berries from the freezer. Both work great. Or, if you're feeling impatient, just scoop it out warm and top with vanilla ice cream (or non-dairy ice cream) for a delicious, if less tidy, fruit dessert.

MAKES 9–12 BARS; COOK TIME: 40–45 MINUTES

Gluten-free rolled oats	5.5 oz / 1½ cups
Brown rice flour	8.25 oz / 1½ cups
Tapioca starch	1.5 oz / ⅓ cup
Brown sugar	9 oz / 1¼ cups
Kosher salt	½ tsp
Baking soda	½ tsp
Chopped walnuts	2 oz / ½ cup
Ground cinnamon	½ tsp
Coconut oil, melted	6 oz / ¾ cup
Fruit preserves	9 oz / ¾ cup
Fresh or frozen berries	10 oz / 2 cups

1 Preheat the oven to 375°F. Line a 9 x 9-inch pan with foil. Spray the foil with baking spray and line the foil with parchment, cut to fit the size of the pan with a 1-inch overhang on all sides. The overhang will allow you to lift the bars out of the pan cleanly and the parchment will keep the bars from sticking to the foil.

2 Put rolled oats, brown rice flour, tapioca starch, brown sugar, salt, baking soda, walnuts, and cinnamon in a large bowl. Toss with your hands or a wooden spoon to combine. Add coconut oil and mix, using your hands or a wooden spoon, until the crumble mixture holds together in large clumps.

3 Spread two thirds of the crumble mixture in the bottom of the pan and press down firmly to create an even layer, making sure the mixture reaches into the corners as well. Spread the fruit preserves over the crust, leaving ½ inch of space around the edges. Scatter the berries over the jam. Sprinkle with the remaining crumble, leaving space so that the berries show through.

4 Bake for 40–45 minutes, rotating between upper and lower oven racks halfway through baking, until the bars are golden brown and the berries are bubbling. Allow to cool completely in the pan before transferring to the refrigerator to chill for at least 2 hours before cutting the bars.

Note: Keep the crumble recipe handy as it's a great topping for all manner of fresh fruit. I make a large batch of the crumble topping and store it in a zip-top bag in my freezer. Toss whatever type of fresh or frozen fruit you have on hand with a little tapioca starch, sugar, and lemon juice. Place the fruit in a baking dish, top with the crumble, and bake it for a perfect fruit crisp in no time!

VEGAN TAHINI & HALVAH BROWNIES

These brownies have become a cult favorite at our bakeshops. They are my gluten-free take on Charlotte Druckman's *New York Times* recipe. They were a little slow to catch on and we received lots of questions in the beginning, mostly "What is halvah?" If you don't know, halvah is a Middle Eastern sesame candy and it's addictively delicious. It's sort of like a whipped, sweet tahini with a flossy, crumbly texture that melts in your mouth. Here, we stir the halvah in gently by hand at the end so it doesn't break up too much. You'll be rewarded with chunks of sesame goodness throughout each piece.

MAKES 9–12 BROWNIES; COOK TIME: 45–50 MINUTES

Whole pitted dates	4 oz / ⅔ cup
Boiling water	8 oz / 1 cup
Coconut oil, melted	5.25 oz / ¾ cup
Unsweetened almond milk	6 oz / ¾ cup
Maple syrup	5.5 oz / ½ cup
Coconut sugar (or brown sugar)	5.5 oz / ¾ cup
Tahini	4.5 oz / ½ cup
Vanilla extract	1½ tsp
White rice flour	3.75 oz / ¾ cup
Sorghum flour	3.75 oz / ¾ cup
Cocoa powder	2.25 oz / ¾ cup
Xanthan gum	½ tsp
Baking powder	1½ tsp
Kosher salt	½ tsp
Chocolate chips	4 oz / ⅔ cup
Halvah, crumbled	3 oz / ½ cup
Sesame seeds	1½ tsp
Large coconut flakes	1 oz / ½ cup
Maldon salt (or coarse salt)	1½ tsp

1 Preheat the oven to 325°F. Line a 9 x 9-inch pan with foil. Spray the foil with baking spray and line the foil with parchment, cut to fit the size of the pan with a 1-inch overhang on all sides. The overhang will allow you to lift the bars out of the pan cleanly and the parchment will keep the bars from sticking to the foil.

2 Place the dates in a small bowl and cover them with boiling water. Set aside for 5–10 minutes until the dates have softened. Drain all the water from the dates.

3 In the bowl of a food processor, blend the softened dates and the melted coconut oil, almond milk, maple syrup, coconut sugar, tahini, and vanilla until the mixture is smooth, 4–5 minutes. You may never get it perfectly smooth but don't worry, a couple of date chunks is just fine.

CONTINUED

4 In the bowl of a stand mixer fitted with the paddle attachment, combine white rice flour, sorghum flour, cocoa powder, xanthan gum, baking powder, and kosher salt. Mix on low speed until well blended, about 1 minute. Pour in the date mixture from the bowl of the food processor and mix on low speed until smooth and evenly distributed, about 2 minutes. Using a spatula, gently stir in the chocolate chips and crumbled halvah so as not to break up the halvah pieces.

5 Pour the batter into the prepared pan and smooth the top with a spatula, making sure the batter reaches all the way into the corners. Sprinkle the top with sesame seeds and coconut flakes. Cover the pan with foil and bake for 40 minutes. Remove foil and bake for another 10–15 minutes, until the middle of the brownies is set and the coconut is golden brown. Remove from the oven and immediately sprinkle with finishing salt. Cool completely before cutting. Bars will keep, tightly wrapped in plastic, in the refrigerator for up to 5 days.

SUPER LEMONY LEMON BARS

I find lemon bars in general to be cloyingly sweet. What I want from a lemon bar is a buttery shortbread crust, a puckery filling that is bright yellow and well-gelled, and a crispy top—all of which is harder to find than you'd think! These bars have all of those important elements. I hope they will become a staple of your everyday baking repertoire.

MAKES 9–12 BARS; COOK TIME: 55–60 MINUTES

FOR THE SHORTBREAD CRUST:

Butter, melted	4 oz / 1 stick
White sugar	1.75 oz / ¼ cup
Vanilla extract	1 tsp
Kosher salt	½ tsp
Brown rice flour	5.5 oz / 1 cup
Tapioca starch	1.08 oz / ¼ cup
Xanthan gum	½ tsp

FOR THE LEMON FILLING:

White sugar	14 oz / 2 cups
Brown rice flour	2.25 oz / ½ cup
Eggs	6 large
Lemon zest	1½ tsp, from 1 lemon
Lemon juice	8 oz / 1 cup, from about 6 lemons

Powdered sugar, for dusting (optional)

1 Preheat the oven to 375°F. Line a 9 x 9-inch pan with foil. Spray the foil with baking spray and line the foil with parchment, cut to fit the size of the pan with a 1-inch overhang on all sides. The overhang will allow you to lift the bars out of the pan cleanly and the parchment will keep the bars from sticking to the foil.

2 Make the crust: In the bowl of a stand mixer fitted with the paddle attachment, mix together the melted butter and white sugar on low speed until just combined, about 1 minute. Add vanilla and mix briefly to combine. Add salt, brown rice flour, tapioca starch, and xanthan gum to the bowl and mix on medium speed until a dough forms and pulls away from the sides of the bowl, about 2 minutes. Using your hands, press the mixture evenly into the bottom of your prepared pan, making sure to get all the way into the corners. It won't look like enough dough at first, but trust me, it will fill the bottom of the pan. Bake the crust for 30–35 minutes, rotating the pan halfway through baking.

CONTINUED

3 While the crust bakes, make the filling: In the same mixer bowl, this time fitted with the whisk attachment, whisk together the sugar and brown rice flour. Add the eggs, lemon zest, and lemon juice all at once and whisk on medium speed until the eggs are well incorporated and the mixture is smooth, about 3 minutes.

4 The crust is done when the surface is evenly golden brown and feels set when gently pushed with your hand. Remove the pan from the oven and set it aside on a flat, heat-proof surface. Reduce the oven temperature to 325°F. Quickly re-whisk the filling to make sure the sugar hasn't sunk to the bottom. Pour the filling into the hot crust base and smooth the top. Carefully move the pan to the oven and bake for 25–30 minutes, until the filling is set when the pan is gently jiggled.

5 Allow the bars to cool completely at room temperature before cutting them (see tip this page). Dust the top with powdered sugar, if desired, before serving. Bars will keep, well wrapped in plastic, in the refrigerator for up to 3 days.

How to cut perfectly clean bars: The best way to get those pretty, clean edges is to use a large, hot, wet knife. Make one long sweeping motion with the tip of the knife, starting at the edge farthest away from you and pulling back toward you, lifting the knife out cleanly when you reach the edge closest to you. Wipe and wet the knife again before making another cut.

PUMPKIN CHEESECAKE BARS WITH GINGER COOKIE CRUST

Making good cheesecake is actually very simple provided you follow three key steps each time. 1) Make sure your cream cheese is very soft in order to combine smoothly with the other ingredients. 2) You must scrape down the bowl between additions of ingredients and make sure all ingredients are truly smooth and fully incorporated before moving on to the next step. 3) Having a plastic paddle with rubber edges for your stand mixer (a "beater blade") is extremely helpful for ensuring a smooth filling every time. If you don't have one, I'd suggest using the whisk attachment instead.

MAKES 9–12 BARS; COOK TIME: 45–50 MINUTES

FOR THE COOKIE CRUST:

Ginger Cookies (page 66; through Step 5)	6 crushed / 1 cup of crumbs
Butter, melted	2 oz / ¼ cup

FOR THE PUMPKIN CHEESECAKE:

Cream cheese, very soft	16 oz / 2 packages
White sugar	3.5 oz / ½ cup
Vanilla extract	2 tsp
Tapioca starch	1½ TB
Pumpkin puree	1 (15-oz) can / 1½ cups
Ground cinnamon	2 tsp
Ground nutmeg	¼ tsp
Ground cardamom	1 tsp
Ground ginger	1 tsp
Heavy cream	6 oz / ¾ cup
Eggs	3 large

1 Preheat the oven to 350°F. Line a 9 x 9-inch pan with foil. Spray the foil with baking spray and line the foil with parchment, cut to fit the size of the pan with a 1-inch overhang on all sides. The overhang will allow you to lift the bars out of the pan cleanly and the parchment will keep the bars from sticking to the foil.

2 Make the crust: In the bowl of a food processor, grind the pre-baked ginger cookies for about 30 seconds until they resemble fine crumbs. Add the melted butter all at once to the processor bowl and pulse until the mixture just holds together (think graham cracker crust). Press the cookie crumb mixture into your prepared pan, pushing it out evenly with your fingers all the way to the corners and edges of the pan. Bake for 25 minutes, rotating the pan halfway through baking. When the crust is baked, set aside to cool.

3 While the crust is cooling, make the filling: In the bowl of a stand mixer fitted with a plastic paddle "beater blade" attachment (or a whisk), cream together soft cream cheese and sugar on high speed until very smooth and no lumps remain, about 3 minutes. Add vanilla and mix briefly, just to combine.

4 Add tapioca starch and continue mixing for about 1 minute until no lumps remain. Add pumpkin puree and cinnamon, nutmeg, cardamom, and ginger and mix on medium speed for 3–4 minutes until smooth. Scrape down the bowl and mix again. With the mixer running on low, add the heavy cream in a slow, steady stream until fully combined.

5 Lastly, add the eggs, one at a time, with the mixer on low speed. Make sure each egg is fully incorporated before adding the next. Take extra care with the eggs. We add these last for a reason. Overmixing the eggs will cause your filling to soufflé (it puffs up really high in the oven, then falls and cracks). Mixing them on a lower and slower setting will result in a more even bake, with a smoother surface and fewer cracks.

6 When your filling is smooth, pour it into the pre-baked cookie crust. Reduce the oven temperature to 325°F and bake for 20–25 minutes until the filling barely jiggles when gently jostled. Be careful not to over-bake or the filling will crack. You want the filling set but still pale in color, with just a slight golden color around the edge. If the filling is browning but still not set, cover the pan with foil and bake a few minutes longer.

7 Cool completely before cutting the bars using the lemon bar cutting method (page 80). Chill before serving. Bars will keep, tightly wrapped in plastic, in the refrigerator for up to 3 days.

PUMPKIN CHEESECAKE BARS WITH
GINGER COOKIE CRUST

RASPBERRY CHEESECAKE BARS WITH CHOCOLATE SHORTBREAD CRUST

Raspberry cheesecake is so pretty! But these bars are more than just pretty. The raspberry puree not only adds lovely color but a great punchy flavor that breaks through the rich filling and leaves you wanting more. The dark cocoa shortbread base is a variation of our lemon bar crust (page 79) and pairs perfectly with the fruity filling. Make these for Valentine's Day or any day you want to spoil your special someone.

MAKES 9–12 BARS; COOK TIME: 45–50 MINUTES

FOR THE CHOCOLATE SHORTBREAD CRUST:

Butter, melted	4 oz / 1 stick
White sugar	1.75 oz / ¼ cup
Vanilla extract	1 tsp
Kosher salt	½ tsp
Brown rice flour	5.5 oz / 1 cup
Cocoa powder	1 oz / ⅓ cup
Xanthan gum	½ tsp

FOR THE RASPBERRY CHEESECAKE:

White sugar	5.25 oz / ¾ cup, divided
Frozen raspberries, defrosted	4.4 oz / 1 cup
Cream cheese, very soft	16 oz / 2 packages
Vanilla extract	2 tsp
Tapioca starch	1½ TB
Heavy cream	6 oz / ¾ cup
Eggs	3 large

1 Preheat the oven to 350°F. Line a 9 x 9-inch pan with foil. Spray the foil with baking spray and line the foil with parchment, cut to fit the size of the pan with a 1-inch overhang on all sides. The overhang will allow you to lift the bars out of the pan cleanly and the parchment will keep the bars from sticking to the foil.

2 Make the crust: In the bowl of a stand mixer fitted with the paddle attachment, cream together the melted butter and sugar on medium speed for 3–4 minutes. Add vanilla and mix briefly to combine. Add salt, brown rice flour, cocoa powder, and xanthan gum and mix together until a dough forms and pulls away from the sides of the bowl. Using your hands, press the mixture evenly into the bottom of your prepared pan, making sure to get all the way into the corners. Bake the crust for 30 minutes, rotating the pan halfway through baking. Set aside to cool at room temperature while you mix the filling.

3 Make the cheesecake: Using a blender or food processor, combine ¼ cup of the sugar and the defrosted raspberries to form a puree, about 2 minutes. You can strain out the seeds or not, depending on your preference. Personally, I don't mind seeds but the filling will be less smooth if you choose to leave them in. Set your puree aside while you mix the rest of the filling.

4 Meanwhile, in the bowl of a stand mixer fitted with the plastic paddle "beater blade" attachment (or whisk), cream together the soft cream cheese and remaining ½ cup sugar on high speed until very smooth and no lumps remain, about 3 minutes. Add vanilla and mix to combine.

5 Add tapioca starch and mix until no lumps remain, about 2 minutes. Add in the raspberry puree and continue mixing until evenly combined, another 2–3 minutes. With the mixer running on low, add the heavy cream a little bit at a time. Continue this way until all of the cream has been added and the mixture is silky smooth.

6 Lastly, add the eggs, one at a time, making sure each egg is fully incorporated before adding the next. See instructions for adding eggs on page 83, step 5.

7 When your filling is smooth, pour it into the pre-baked cookie crust. Reduce the oven temperature to 325°F and bake for 20–25 minutes until the filling barely jiggles when gently jostled. If the filling is browning but still not set, cover the pan with foil and bake a few minutes longer.

8 Cool the bars completely before cutting them using the lemon bar cutting method (see page 80). Chill before serving. Bars will keep tightly wrapped in plastic in the refrigerator for up to 3 days.

Note: These bars look especially nice when drizzled with Bittersweet Chocolate Ganache (page 95). Using any drizzling method you like, either tidy with a piping bag or "abstract" using a spoon, drizzle the ganache onto the cooled bars and chill again before cutting them.

MAPLE-WHISKEY PECAN PIE BARS WITH SHORTBREAD CRUST

These tasty bars are like your favorite pecan pie, but in bar form. They use the same basic shortbread crust recipe as our Super Lemony Lemon Bars (page 79). Some type of alcohol is really important to balance the sweetness of the filling but a shot of espresso can be substituted to great effect as well. If you're shy about corn syrup or can't find dark corn syrup at the store, you can substitute brown rice syrup, available at most natural foods stores, in the same quantity as the dark corn syrup. The flavor will be slightly more roasted but the bars will still be excellent.

MAKES 9–12 BARS; COOK TIME: 50–60 MINUTES

FOR THE SHORTBREAD CRUST:

Butter, melted	4 oz / 1 stick
White sugar	1.75 oz / ¼ cup
Vanilla extract	1 tsp
Kosher salt	½ tsp
Brown rice flour	5.5 oz / 1 cup
Tapioca starch	1.08 oz / ¼ cup
Xanthan gum	½ tsp

FOR THE PECAN PIE FILLING:

Eggs	4 large
White sugar	7 oz / 1 cup
Whiskey	1 oz / 2 TB
Vanilla extract	1 tsp
Dark corn syrup (or brown rice syrup)	5.5 oz / ½ cup
Maple syrup	5.5 oz / ½ cup
Butter, melted	2 oz / ½ stick
Chopped raw pecans	4 oz / 1 cup

1 Preheat the oven to 350°F. Line a 9 x 9-inch pan with foil. Spray the foil with baking spray and line the foil with parchment, cut to fit the size of the pan with a 1-inch overhang on all sides. The overhang will allow you to lift the bars out of the pan cleanly and the parchment will keep the filling from sticking to the foil.

2 Make the crust: In the bowl of a stand mixer fitted with the paddle attachment, cream together the melted butter and sugar on medium speed for 3–4 minutes. Add the vanilla and mix briefly to combine. Add the salt, brown rice flour, tapioca starch, and xanthan gum and mix together on medium speed until a dough forms and pulls away from the sides of the bowl, about 3 minutes more. Using your hands, press the mixture evenly into the bottom of your prepared pan, making sure to get all the way into the corners. Bake the crust for 25–30 minutes, rotating the pan halfway through baking, until it is evenly golden brown. Set aside to cool at room temperature while you make the filling.

3 Make the filling: In a large mixing bowl, whisk together eggs, sugar, whiskey, and vanilla by hand. (Note: You can certainly do this step in a stand mixer fitted with the whisk attachment, but I find with this small quantity, sometimes the whisk doesn't reach the bottom of the bowl and the filling does not get well blended.) Add the corn syrup and maple syrup and whisk until the mixture is smooth. Add the melted butter and whisk to combine. Finally, stir in the chopped pecans.

4 Reduce the oven temperature to 325°F. Pour the filling over the cooled crust. Carefully return the pan to the oven and bake for 30–35 minutes until the filling is well puffed up and it just starts to crack around the edges. The filling will be very liquidy when you remove it from the oven, but don't worry: It will set as it cools.

5 Chill the bars in the refrigerator for at least 2 hours or overnight before cutting using the lemon bar cutting method (see page 80). Bars will keep, tightly wrapped in plastic, in the refrigerator for up to 5 days or in the freezer for up to 1 month.

CASUAL CAKES

Orange Polenta Cake

Bittersweet Chocolate Ganache

Lemon Angel Food Cake

Summer Berry Upside-Down Cake

Ricotta Cake with Strawberry-Rhubarb Crumble

Flourless Chocolate-Almond Torte

Spicy Gingerbread Cake

ORANGE POLENTA CAKE

On a recent trip to the UK, I saw a version of this cake in nearly every sweet shop we popped into. Since it was one of the only cakes that was gluten-free just about everywhere, it became my go-to treat during our stay. I had it soaked with a citrus syrup, topped with fresh fruit, and petite versions sandwiched with chantilly cream. Upon my arrival home, I immediately started working out the recipe until I got it just right, and then I topped it with a crown of creamy melted chocolate. It has since become far and away our best-selling cake at the bakeshops and a daily staple of our pastry display.

The key to this recipe is using instant polenta, which can be tricky to locate but I've found Moretti Lampo (instant) polenta at well-stocked specialty markets or online. The instant polenta lends a nice cornmeal crunch to the finished cake. If you substitute standard polenta, the recipe will still work but the cake will be crunchier in the end.

SERVES 8; COOK TIME: 40–45 MINUTES

Butter, soft	8 oz / 2 sticks
White sugar	7 oz / 1 cup
Eggs	3 large
Orange zest	1 TB / from 1 large orange
Vanilla extract	1 tsp
Almond meal	7.6 oz / 2¼ cups
Instant polenta	2.9 oz / ½ cup
Baking powder	1 tsp
Kosher salt	1 tsp
Xanthan gum	½ tsp
Bittersweet Chocolate Ganache (page 95)	½ cup

1 Preheat the oven to 325°F. Spray an 8-inch round cake pan with cooking spray and line the bottom with a parchment circle. Spray the parchment circle with cooking spray as well.

2 In the bowl of a stand mixer fitted with the paddle attachment, cream together the soft butter and sugar on medium speed until the mixture is light and fluffy and pale in color, about 3 minutes. Add eggs, one at a time, and mix on low speed, scraping down the bowl between additions. Add orange zest and vanilla and mix until all the ingredients are well combined.

3 Add almond meal, instant polenta, baking powder, salt, and xanthan gum to the mixer bowl and mix on medium speed, stopping the mixer to scrape down the bowl once or twice, until the batter is creamy and pale in color, about 2–3 minutes.

CONTINUED

4 Pour the batter into the prepared cake pan and, using a small offset spatula or rubber spatula, smooth out the top and spread the batter all the way to the sides of the pan.

5 Bake for 40–45 minutes, rotating the pan halfway through baking, until the top of the cake is evenly golden brown and feels set. When finished the cake will just start to pull away from the sides of the pan but will feel still somewhat soft when pressed gently in the center.

6 Let cool completely in the pan on a wire rack. In the meantime, make the bittersweet chocolate ganache. When the cake has cooled, invert it onto a pedestal or platter and remove the parchment circle.

7 To apply the ganache, start with a 3-inch wide dollop of warm, pourable ganache in the center of the cooled cake. Use the back of a spoon or an offset spatula to spread the ganache almost to the edge of the cake, without going over the sides. Allow the ganache to set before slicing the cake.
The cake will keep, wrapped tightly in plastic wrap, in the refrigerator up to 3 days.

BITTERSWEET CHOCOLATE GANACHE

One of the simplest, most versatile recipes to use for all sorts of occasions. Enjoy this ganache thickly spread on the top of the Orange Polenta Cake (page 92), or drizzle it over the Raspberry Cheesecake Bars with Chocolate Crust (page 86), or simply spoon it over ice cream for a luxurious chocolate sauce.

MAKES ABOUT 2 CUPS; COOK TIME: 5 MINUTES

Bittersweet chocolate, chopped	8 oz / 1¼ cups
Heavy cream	12 oz / 1½ cups
Vanilla extract or liqueur of choice	½ oz / 1 TB

1 Place the chopped chocolate in a medium bowl.

2 In a mircowave-safe bowl, microwave the cream at full power for about 2 minutes, until steaming hot but not yet boiling. Pour the hot cream over the chopped chocolate and add the vanilla. Allow to sit for 2–3 minutes until the hot cream melts the chocolate. Whisk the chocolate and cream together until smooth and glossy. Use immediately or cover and refrigerate for up to 3 days. Allow the ganache to return to room temperature and whisk until smooth before using.

LEMON ANGEL FOOD CAKE

Flavored with lemon two ways, this zesty citrus cake makes a perfect base for fresh berries and whipped cream. It's also great served unadorned and is the perfect make-ahead cake for Easter or Mother's Day brunch as it's not too sweet, goes great with tea or mimosas, and becomes even more moist the next day.

SERVES 8–10; COOK TIME: 40–45 MINUTES

Eggs, separated	8 large
White sugar	7 oz / 1 cup, divided
Lemon zest	1 TB, from 1 large lemon
Lemon juice	2 oz / ¼ cup, from 2 lemons
Unsweetened almond milk	4 oz / ½ cup
Almond meal	13.5 oz / 4 cups
Baking powder	2 tsp
Kosher salt	2 tsp
Xanthan gum	1 tsp
Powdered sugar, for finishing	

1 Preheat the oven to 325°F. Spray a 10-cup tube pan with a removable bottom with cooking spray.

2 In the bowl of a stand mixer fitted with the whisk attachment, whisk the egg whites on high speed until foamy, 2–3 minutes. Slowly sprinkle in 1.75 oz / ¼ cup of sugar and continue whisking on high until stiff peaks form, 3–4 minutes more. Set aside while you mix the egg yolks.

3 In a large mixing bowl, combine egg yolks, the remaining 5.25 oz / ¾ cup sugar, lemon zest, lemon juice, and almond milk. Whisk by hand until emulsified. Add the almond meal, baking powder, salt, and xanthan gum and whisk until a thick, smooth paste forms.

4 Using a large spatula, fold one third of the whipped egg whites into the yolk mixture to lighten the mixture slightly. Carefully fold in the remaining whipped egg whites, gently lifting and folding until the mixture is uniform in color and texture.

5 Gently place the batter into the prepared tube pan, spreading it out evenly and smoothing the surface. Bake for 40–45 minutes, rotating the pan halfway through baking, until the cake is golden brown and puffed up. Don't worry if the cake deflates a bit as it cools.

6 Let the cake cool completely in the pan before unmolding. To unmold, run a small offset spatula between the cake and the pan. Lift the cake out of the pan, leaving the removable bottom attached. Run your spatula between the cake and the center post and invert the cake onto a pedestal or serving platter. Dust with powdered sugar and serve at room temperature. Cake keeps on the counter, wrapped well in plastic wrap, for up to 3 days.

SUMMER BERRY UPSIDE-DOWN CAKE

This is such a pretty and old-fashioned cake. The fresh, bursting fruit and light, vanilla-flecked cake make this a perfect anytime dessert. I generally make it in the summer when I have an assortment of fresh berries available, but you can really make it any time of year. It would be wonderful with pears or apples in the fall or fresh cranberries in the winter.

Do not be afraid to invert the cake. If the fruit sticks to the pan, just press it back onto the surface and no one will ever know the difference. The key here is to make sure you unmold the cake while it's still warm so that the fruit releases before the sugar crystallizes. When the pan is just cool enough to touch it's the right time to invert the cake.

SERVES 6–8; COOK TIME: 40–45 MINUTES

FOR THE FRUIT & CARAMEL:

Butter, soft	2 oz / ½ stick
Lemon juice	1 TB
White sugar	3.5 oz / ½ cup
Kosher salt	½ tsp
Fresh mixed berries	7.5 oz / 1½ cups
Lemon zest	1 TB, from 1 large lemon

FOR THE CAKE:

Butter, soft	4 oz / 1 stick
White sugar	7 oz / 1 cup
Eggs	2 large
Vanilla paste	1 TB
White rice flour	3.5 oz / ¾ cup
Brown rice flour	2.75 oz / ½ cup
Tapioca starch	1.25 oz / ¼ cup
Xanthan gum	¾ tsp
Baking powder	1½ tsp
Baking soda	½ tsp
Kosher salt	½ tsp
Buttermilk	4 oz / ½ cup
Unsweetened whipped cream or vanilla ice cream, for serving	

1 Preheat the oven to 325°F. Spray an 8-inch round cake pan with cooking spray and line the bottom with a parchment circle. Spray the parchment circle with cooking spray as well.

2 Prepare the fruit and caramel: Combine the soft butter, lemon juice, sugar, and salt in a small microwave-safe bowl. Heat in the microwave until sugar is dissolved, butter is melted, and the caramel is bubbly, about 90 seconds. Set aside.

3 Meanwhile, in a small bowl combine berries and lemon zest. Pour the caramel into the of the prepared pan so it covers the bottom. Top with the berries in an even layer. Set aside.

CONTINUED

4 Make the cake: In the bowl of a stand mixer fitted with the paddle attachment, cream together the soft butter and sugar on medium-high speed until light and fluffy, about 2 minutes. Agg eggs and vanilla paste and scrape down the sides of the bowl. Continue mixing for 2–3 minutes until eggs are fully incorporated. Add white rice flour, brown rice flour, tapioca starch, xanthan gum, baking powder, baking soda, and salt and continue to mix until the batter is smooth and pale in color, about 3 minutes more. With the machine on low, slowly stream in the butter-milk. Mix on medium speed until the batter is pale and creamy, 1–2 minutes.

5 Using a spatula, scrape the cake batter into the prepared pan over of the berries. Spread the batter into an even layer, reaching all the way to the edges of the pan.

6 Cover with foil and bake for 20 minutes. Rotate the pan and remove the foil. Continue baking for another 20–25 minutes until the cake is set and the edges are a golden brown color. The berries should be bubbling up around the edges just slightly.

7 Let cool in the pan on a wire rack until the pan is just cool enough to touch. Run a small offset spatula between the cake and the sides of the pan. Invert onto a pedestal or platter and press any berries that may have stuck in the pan back onto the top of the cake. Serve with unsweetened whipped cream or vanilla ice cream.

RICOTTA CAKE WITH STRAWBERRY-RHUBARB CRUMBLE

I developed this recipe for our Easter menu at the bakery after reading a recipe for a strawberry crumble cake in *Sweet* by Yotam Ottolenghi and Helen Goh, which is such a beautiful and inspiring book, and a recipe for a citrus ricotta cake from Liz Prueitt of Tartine. I combined the two ideas into this one festive cake. Rhubarb is just coming into season around Easter in California and it's also a favorite of my husband's. So, I combined those two ideas into this one cake and it was met with rave reviews. It's now a springtime staple at our bakeshops and I hope it will also become a staple at your table.

SERVES 6–8; COOK TIME: 45–50 MINUTES

FOR THE STRAWBERRY-RHUBARB CRUMBLE:

Crumble Topping (page 74, step 2)	10 oz / 1½ cups
Fresh strawberries, hulled and quartered	5 oz / 1 cup
Fresh rhubarb, sliced ¼ inch thick	4.5 oz / 1 cup
White sugar	3.5 oz / ½ cup
Orange zest	1½ tsp, from ½ orange
Vanilla extract	1½ tsp

FOR THE CAKE:

Butter, soft	4 oz / 1 stick
White sugar	5 oz / ¾ cup, divided
Eggs, separated	5 large
Whole milk ricotta	6 oz / 1 cup
Orange juice	4 oz / ½ cup
Instant polenta	2.9 oz / ½ cup
Almond meal	4 oz / 1¼ cups
Tapioca starch	1.25 oz / ¼ cup
Kosher salt	½ tsp
Xanthan gum	½ tsp

1 Preheat the oven to 325°F. Spray an 8-inch round cake pan with cooking spray and line the bottom with a parchment circle.

2 Make the strawberry-rhubarb crumble: Prepare the crumble and set aside. In a medium bowl, toss together strawberries, rhubarb, sugar, orange zest, and vanilla. Set the fruit aside to macerate while you prepare the cake batter.

3 Make the cake: In the bowl of a stand mixer fitted with the paddle attachment, cream together the soft butter and 3 oz / ½ cup of the sugar on medium-high speed until light and fluffy, about 2 minutes. Add egg yolks, ricotta, and orange juice and continue mixing until the mixture is smooth, 1–2 minutes more. Scrape down the bowl with a spatula. Add polenta, almond meal, tapioca starch, salt, and xanthan gum and mix for 2–3 minutes until the egg yolk and flour mixture is smooth and well combined. Scrape into a large bowl and set aside.

CONTINUED

4 Rinse out the mixer bowl and dry it well. Fit the bowl with the whisk attachment and whip the egg whites on high speed until foamy, 2–3 minutes. Slowly stream in the remaining 2 oz / ¼ cup sugar and whisk until stiff peaks form, 3–4 minutes more.

5 Add one third of the egg white and sugar mixture to the egg yolk and flour mixture and mix with a spatula to combine. Add the remaining two thirds of the egg white mixture and fold it into the batter carefully, taking care not to deflate the egg whites. Fold until the mixture is a light golden color. It's ok if some streaks of white remain. It's better to have the batter less mixed than to overmix and deflate.

6 Place the prepared pan on a baking sheet and carefully spread the batter into the cake pan. Scatter the fruit mixture on top of the batter and sprinkle the crumble over the fruit. If you have any extra crumble, freeze it in a zip-top plastic bag for your next cake. Bake the cake on the baking sheet for 45–50 minutes, rotating the baking sheet halfway through, until fruit is bubbly, the sides are golden brown, and the cake is nicely puffed up in the center. The center will still feel quite soft to the touch. Don't worry, it will set as the cake cools. Do not be tempted to overbake. You want the cooled cake to have a tender, cheesecake-like texture when sliced.

7 Let the cake cool completely in the pan. When ready to unmold, carefully run an offset spatula between the cake and the side of the pan. Invert a plate onto the top of the cake and flip the cake out (crumble side down). Remove the parchment circle from the bottom and place your cake pedestal or serving platter on the underside of the cake. Flip the cake over again so the crumble side is now facing up and remove the inverted plate. Your cake is ready to serve!

FLOURLESS CHOCOLATE-ALMOND TORTE

I developed this recipe to sell at our bakeshops during Hanukkah. I wanted a flourless chocolate torte that could be baked in a regular cake pan, rather than a springform. This torte has a rich yet light, cloud-like texture. Dusted with a snowfall of powdered sugar or served with a dollop of whipped crème fraîche, it is the ultimate in simple elegance. It's perfect for Hanukkah, Passover, or any time of year when you're craving a decadent chocolate ending to a special meal.

SERVES 6–8; COOK TIME: 30–40 MINUTES

Almond paste, soft	7 oz / 1 tube
Butter	3 oz / ¾ stick
Eggs	3 large
Cocoa powder	1.5 oz / ½ cup
Kosher salt	½ tsp
Egg whites	3 oz / 3 large whites
White sugar	2 TB
Powered sugar or cocoa powder, for finishing	
Cocoa Nib Cream (page 20; optional)	

1 Preheat the oven to 325°F. Spray a 9-inch round cake pan with nonstick spray and line the bottom with parchment. In the microwave on high power, soften the almond paste and butter in a microwave-safe bowl until they both reach spreadable consistency, about 90 seconds.

2 In the bowl of a stand mixer fitted with the paddle attachment, mix together the softened almond paste and butter at medium speed until smooth. With the mixer running on low speed, add the whole eggs, one at a time, and mix until the mixture is very smooth and the eggs are well combined. Add cocoa powder and salt and continue mixing on low speed until the mixture is homogeneous, about 2 minutes more. Transfer the almond-cocoa mixture to a large mixing bowl and set aside.

3 Clean the mixer bowl well and fit your mixer with the whisk attachment. Beat egg whites on high until foamy, 2–3 minutes. Slowly sprinkle in the sugar and mix on high until stiff peaks form, 3–4 minutes more.

CONTINUED

4 Using a large rubber spatula, fold one third of the beaten egg whites into the almond-cocoa mixture until combined. You don't have to be too thorough on this first addition. The idea is to bring the almond-cocoa mixture to a similar consistency as the egg whites so the remainder of the egg whites fold in easily without deflating.

5 Add the remaining two thirds of the beaten egg whites all at once to the large bowl. Carefully fold egg whites into the almond-cocoa mixture, taking care not to deflate the whites while mixing. Once the egg whites are nicely folded in and no white streaks remain, pour the batter into the prepared cake pan. Gently level off the top using a small offset spatula.

6 Bake for 30–40 minutes, until the torte is puffed up and feels set but not completely solid in the center. Allow to cool in the pan at least 30 minutes before inverting onto a serving platter. Don't worry if the cake sinks a bit as it cools. That is normal and it will still be delicious. Sprinkle with powdered sugar or cocoa powder before serving. If desired, serve with Cocoa Nib Cream (page 20).

SPICY GINGERBREAD CAKE

I adore gingerbread cake! To me, nothing evokes the holidays more. It's like Christmas in every bite. This cake is adapted from Helen Goh's recipe in *Sweet* and is the very best I've ever had. It's a delicate, tender cake that is a delight on its own and really needs no adornment. But, it's great with a dollop of unsweetened whipped cream or crème fraîche and looks particularly festive sprinkled with powdered sugar.

SERVES 8–10; COOK TIME: 30–35 MINUTES

Brown sugar	3.75 oz / ¾ cup
Brown rice flour	4 oz / ¾ cup
Millet flour	1.25 oz / ¼ cup
Tapioca starch	1.125 oz / ¼ cup
White rice flour	2.5 oz / ½ cup
Baking soda	1 tsp
Ground cinnamon	1 tsp
Ground ginger	2 tsp
Ground cloves	¼ tsp
Ground nutmeg	¼ tsp
Ground cardamom	½ tsp
Kosher salt	½ tsp
Xanthan gum	½ tsp
Rice bran oil (or vegetable oil)	3.5 oz / ½ cup
Molasses	6 oz / ½ cup
Eggs	2 large
Water	4 oz / ½ cup
Powdered sugar, optional, for dusting	

1 Preheat the oven to 350°F. Spray an 8-inch cake pan with cooking spray and line the bottom with a parchment circle. If using a bundt pan, thoroughly spray the sides and middle post with cooking spray.

2 In the bowl of a stand mixer fitted with the paddle attachment, combine brown sugar, brown rice flour, millet flour, tapioca starch, white rice flour, baking soda, ground cinnamon, ginger, cloves, nutmeg, and cardmom, salt, and xanthan gum on low speed just to combine. Add the oil, molasses, and eggs. Mix briefly on low speed to incorporate, 1–2 minutes. Continue mixing on low speed while slowly drizzling in the water until the batter is smooth and no lumps remain, 2–3 minutes more. Scrape down the sides to make sure all the dry ingredients are fully incorporated.

3 Pour the cake batter into the prepared pan and bake for 30–35 minutes until the top is just set and the middle no longer jiggles when jostled. Transfer to a wire rack to cool completely. Invert onto a pedestal or platter when ready to serve. Lightly dust with powdered sugar (optional) before serving.

MULTI-LAYER CAKES & ICINGS

Mom's Classic Carrot Cake

Vanilla Bean Cream Cheese Icing

Chocolate-Orange Layer Cake

Vegan Chocolate–Olive Oil Layer Cake

Vegan Buttercream

Whipped Chocolate Ganache Icing

Chocolate Chip Banana Cake

Strawberry & Meringue Layer Cake with Whipped Cream

MOM'S CLASSIC CARROT CAKE

This was one of the things my mom made when I was growing up that I absolutely loved! I requested it for every birthday that I can remember. This is a homey cake but looks so appealing sandwiched with a thick layer of Vanilla Bean Cream Cheese Icing (page 113). When decorating, I leave the sides of this cake "naked," as I like seeing the bits of carrots and walnuts showing through, but I don't skip a thick swoosh of icing on the top.

SERVES 8–10; COOK TIME: 40–45 MINUTES

Vegetable oil	8.75 oz / 1¼ cups
White sugar	14 oz / 2 cups
Eggs	4 large
Vanilla extract	1 tsp
White rice flour	7.5 oz / 1½ cups
Brown rice flour	4.125 oz / ¾ cup
Baking soda	1 tsp
Baking powder	2 tsp
Xanthan gum	½ tsp
Ground cinnamon	2 tsp
Ground nutmeg	½ tsp
Ground cardamom	½ tsp
Kosher salt	½ tsp
Shredded carrots	7 oz / 2 cups
Chopped raw walnuts	4 oz / 1 cup
Vanilla Bean Cream Cheese Icing (page 113)	12 oz / 2 cups

1 Preheat the oven to 325°F. Spray two 8-inch round cake pans with cooking spray and line the bottoms with parchment circles.

2 In the bowl of a stand mixer fitted with the paddle attachment, combine oil, sugar, eggs, and vanilla on medium speed until well combined, about 2 minutes, occasionally scraping down the bowl.

3 Add white rice flour, brown rice flour, baking soda, baking powder, xanthan gum, cinnamon, nutmeg, cardamom, and salt to the wet ingredients. Mix on medium speed until smooth, 2–3 minutes. Add carrots and walnuts and mix until all the ingredients are uniformly combined, 1–2 minutes more. Divide the batter evenly between the prepared cake pans.

4 Bake for 40–45 minutes, rotating the pans between the upper and lower oven racks halfway through baking, until the cake is golden brown and the top feels set when pushed very gently with your finger, or a cake tester or toothpick inserted into the center comes out clean. Cool cakes in pans completely and then unmold onto a wire rack before trimming and icing.

5 Using a long serrated knife, carefully trim off the tops of both cakes so the layers are flat on both sides. Place one trimmed cake on a platter facing up, so you're icing the cut side of the cake. Spread on a thick layer of vanilla bean cream cheese icing. Invert the other layer on top, so the bottom of the second cake is facing up. Spread another layer of icing on the top of the cake. You can either frost the sides or leave them naked, depending on how much icing you personally enjoy and how you want the finished cake to look.

VANILLA BEAN CREAM CHEESE ICING

The key to a smooth cream cheese icing, free of pesky lumps, is starting with very soft cream cheese. You want it to be the same consistency as room temperature butter before you begin mixing it. Make sure you mix it thoroughly with the butter before adding the powdered sugar. If your powdered sugar is a bit lumpy, I'd suggest sifting it for maximum smoothness as well.

MAKES ABOUT 5 CUPS, ENOUGH FOR ONE 2-LAYER CAKE; COOK TIME: 10 MINUTES

Cream cheese, soft	16 oz / 2 packages
Butter, soft	8 oz / 2 sticks
Powdered sugar, sifted	24 oz / 3 cups
Vanilla paste	1 TB
Kosher salt	½ tsp

1 In the bowl of a stand mixer fitted with the paddle attachment, mix the cream cheese and butter on medium speed until fully mixed and no lumps remain, 2–3 minutes. Scrape down the sides of the bowl with a spatula. Add powdered sugar, 1 cup at a time, and mix on low speed to start, increasing speed as the sugar is incorporated, for about 4 minutes total. Scrape the bowl after each addition.

2 After all the powdered sugar has been added and the icing is completely smooth and lump-free, add the vanilla paste and salt. Mix briefly to combine.

3 Set the icing aside at room temperature until you're ready to use it. You can make the icing well ahead and store it in the refrigerator but it does set up as it chills. You'll need to soften it in the microwave and re-whip it before applying it to your cake. Otherwise, the icing will be hard and difficult to spread on a fresh cake without tearing it.

VARIATION

Chocolate Cream Cheese Icing: Replace 1 cup of the powdered sugar with 1 cup cocoa powder and add 1 tablespoon fresh orange zest. Replace the 1 tablespoon vanilla paste with 1 teaspoon orange extract or 1 tablespoon orange liqueur, such as Cointreau or Grand Marnier.

CHOCOLATE-ORANGE LAYER CAKE

Chocolate and orange is a classic combination for good reason. The flavors work beautifully together in this light, moist, truly delectable cake. Don't feel like being "fancy" and cutting and icing layers of cake? Not to worry . . . make this cake in a 9 x 13-inch pan instead and generously cover the top with our Chocolate Cream Cheese Icing (page 113) for an easy and festive cake to serve on any weeknight.

SERVES 8–10; COOK TIME: 35–40 MINUTES

White rice flour	5 oz / 1 cup
Sorghum flour	2.25 oz / ½ cup
Tapioca starch	1.25 oz / ¼ cup
Cocoa powder	2 oz / ⅔ cup
White sugar	14 oz / 2 cups
Xanthan gum	½ tsp
Baking powder	1½ tsp
Baking soda	1½ tsp
Kosher salt	1 tsp
Eggs	2 large
Whole milk	8 oz / 1 cup
Coconut oil, melted	3.5 oz / ½ cup
Vanilla extract	1 tsp
Orange extract	2 tsp
Fresh orange juice, hot	8 oz / 1 cup
Chocolate Cream Cheese Icing (page 113)	12 oz / 2 cups

1 Preheat the oven to 325°F. Spray two 8-inch round cake pans with cooking spray and line the bottoms with parchment circles.

2 In the bowl of a stand mixer fitted with the paddle attachment, combine white rice flour, sorghum flour, tapioca starch, cocoa powder, sugar, xanthan gum, baking powder, baking soda, and salt on low speed to combine and to break up any clumps in the cocoa powder.

3 Add eggs, milk, coconut oil, and vanilla and orange extracts and mix on medium speed to combine, about 2 minutes. With the machine running on low speed, slowly drizzle in the hot orange juice until well combined. Adding the hot orange juice here will activate the baking powder and lend a fudgier texture to the finished cake.

4 Divide the batter equally between the prepared cake pans. Bake for 40–45 minutes, rotating the pans between the upper and lower oven racks halfway through baking, until the middle of the cake is springy when touched, or a cake tester or toothpick inserted into the center of the cake comes out clean and the edges just start to pull away from the sides of the pan.

5 Cool cakes in pans completely and then unmold onto a wire rack before before trimming and icing. Using the carrot cake icing method (see page 110), frost the cake with a thick layer of chocolate cream cheese icing.

VEGAN CHOCOLATE–OLIVE OIL LAYER CAKE

This is a rich, moist, super-fudgy cake that anyone, vegan or otherwise, would be delighted to have for their birthday. The addition of coffee brings out the chocolate flavor beautifully. The cake is also quite stable and cuts well when cooled, so you can form lots of thin layers if you prefer a many-layered presentation. We use olive oil here as it lends a fruity background flavor and a nice richness to the finished cake, but any vegetable oil you have on hand will work well.

SERVES 8–10; COOK TIME: 45–50 MINUTES

Brown rice flour	8.25 oz / 1½ cups
White rice flour	7.5 oz / 1½ cups
Cocoa powder	4.5 oz / 1½ cups
White sugar	10.5 oz / 1½ cups
Brown sugar	11 oz / 2 cups
Baking soda	1 TB
Xanthan gum	1 tsp
Kosher salt	1 tsp
Olive oil	7 oz / 1 cup
Warm water	12 oz / 1½ cups
Apple cider vinegar	2 TB
Warm brewed coffee	12 oz / 1½ cups
Vegan Buttercream (page 118)	28 oz / 4 cups

1 Preheat the oven to 325°F. Spray two 8-inch round cake pans with cooking spray and line the bottoms with parchment circles.

2 In the bowl of a stand mixer fitted with the paddle attachment, combine brown rice flour, white rice flour, cocoa powder, both sugars, baking soda, xanthan gum, and salt and mix on low speed. Add olive oil, warm water, and vinegar and mix on low speed for 1–2 minutes until well combined. With the mixer running, slowly drizzle in the warm coffee, a little bit at a time, until all the coffee has been added and the mixture is smooth. Scrape down the sides and bottom of the bowl with a spatula, making sure there are no lingering bits of unmixed dry ingredients on the bottom.

3 Divide the batter evenly between the prepared pans. Bake for 45–50 minutes, rotating the pans between the upper and lower oven racks halfway through baking, until the middle of the cake is springy when touched, or a cake tester or toothpick inserted into the center of the cake comes out clean and the edges just start to pull away from the sides of the pan.

4 Cool cakes in pans completely and then unmold onto a wire rack before before trimming and icing. You can also make the cakes ahead and refrigerate them overnight before assembling.

5 Using a long serrated knife, carefully trim off the top of the cakes so the layers are flat on both sides. Invert one cake onto a platter, so you're icing the bottom of the cake, and spread on a thick layer of vegan buttercream. Sandwich the other layer (also inverted) on top and spread another layer of icing on the top of the cake. You can either frost the sides or leave them naked, depending on your aesthetic preference. Store any leftover cake, tightly wrapped in plastic, in the refrigerator for up to 2 days.

VEGAN BUTTERCREAM

My bakery team worked for a long time to get this vegan icing just right. It's creamy, spreadable, pipable, and everything a proper icing for a celebration cake should be. You can flavor it anyway you like. Our basic vanilla recipe and a chocolate variation are included below but cinnamon, orange zest, or coffee buttercream would all be delicious as well. Selecting the right vegan butter substitute here is key to achieving the proper flavor. I prefer Earth Balance as its flavor is neutral and not too salty. Any non-hydrogenated vegetable shortening will work here but I use Spectrum Naturals.

This icing needs time to set up before spreading it onto your cake. I like to make it right after I put my cakes in the oven, so it has time to set up while the cakes bake and cool. Just give it a quick mix in the stand mixer to aerate it before spreading it onto the cooled cakes.

MAKES ABOUT 5 CUPS; COOK TIME: 10 MINUTES

Vegan butter, soft	8 oz / 2 sticks
Non-hydrogenated vegetable shortening, soft	6.5 oz / 1 cup
Powdered sugar	28 oz / 7 cups
Vanilla paste	1 TB
Kosher salt	½ tsp
Unsweetened nut or plant milk	6 oz / ¾ cup

1 In the bowl of a stand mixer fitted with the paddle attachment, mix together the vegan butter and shortening on medium-high for 2–3 minutes, until completely smooth and no lumps remain. Add in the powdered sugar, 1 cup at a time, starting at a low speed and increasing the speed as each cup is incorporated. Make sure you scrape down the bowl and that no lumps remain before adding the next cup.

2 After all the powdered sugar has been added, mix in the vanilla paste and salt. With the machine running, slowly drizzle in the nut milk until it is fully incorporated and the mixture is smooth. Turn the mixer up to high speed for 1–2 minutes and whip the icing until it's super light and fluffy. Chill in the fridge until ready to use. Extra icing will keep in the refrigerator in an airtight container for up to 1 week.

VARIATION:

Chocolate Vegan Buttercream: Substitute 4 ounces / 1⅓ cups cocoa powder for 4 ounces / 1 cup powdered sugar. Proceed with the same instructions.

WHIPPED CHOCOLATE GANACHE ICING

I struggle to think of a single thing not to love about rich, thick, whipped chocolate ganache icing! Made fresh and still soft, it's perfect for spreading onto any layered cake like our Chocolate Chip Banana Cake (page 121) or our Chocolate-Orange Layer Cake (page 114). If you have any leftovers after icing your cakes, it's also perfect for making chocolate truffles. Just allow the ganache to set up in the fridge and use a spoon or a small ice cream scoop to roll into little balls. Toss them in cocoa powder or powdered sugar and store them in your fridge. They're perfect as a hostess gift or a homemade holiday gift.

MAKES ABOUT 4 CUPS; COOK TIME: ABOUT 5 MINUTES

Heavy cream	18 oz / 2¼ cups
Bittersweet chocolate, chopped	24 oz / 4 cups
Vanilla extract or liqueur of your choice	½ oz / 1 TB

1 Microwave the cream at full power for about 2 minutes, until steaming hot but not yet boiling. Pour the hot cream over the chopped chocolate in a heat-proof bowl and add the vanilla. Allow to sit for 2–3 minutes for the cream to melt the chocolate.

2 Using a whisk, stir the cream and the chocolate together. You should end up with a smooth, shiny, glossy, emulsified mixture that looks like rich chocolate fudge. If you still have unmelted chocolate lumps in your cream, don't worry. Place the whole thing back in the microwave and heat in 30-second intervals, thoroughly whisking between each heating, until the chocolate is fully melted.

3 Allow the ganache to set for about 30 minutes in the refridgerator. You want it to be pliable but not liquid.

4 In the bowl of a stand mixer fitted with the whisk attachment, whisk the ganache on high speed until it looks like chocolatey whipped cream. If the ganache is still too soft to whip into peaks, just place the whole bowl back in the fridge for a few minutes and try again. To frost a cake, the whipped ganache should be used right away, while it's soft enough to spread easily.

CHOCOLATE CHIP BANANA CAKE

This cake is a wonderful staple to have in your arsenal of go-to recipes. It can be a "fancy" layered cake as shown here, presented with a delectable Whipped Chocolate Ganache Icing or baked into a humble loaf pan and sliced for a simple teatime snack.

SERVES 8–10; COOK TIME: 30–35 MINUTES FOR 8-INCH ROUNDS; 55–65 MINUTES FOR 9-INCH LOAVES

Butter, soft	8 oz / 2 sticks
White sugar	14 oz / 2 cups
Eggs	4 large
Ripe bananas, mashed	6 medium
Vanilla extract	2 tsp
Brown rice flour	11 oz / 2 cups
Millet flour	3.5 oz / ¾ cup
Tapioca starch	3 oz / ¾ cup
Baking soda	2 tsp
Kosher salt	1 tsp
Xanthan gum	1 tsp
Sour cream or Greek yogurt	2 oz / ¼ cup
Chocolate chips	9 oz / 1½ cups
Whipped Chocolate Ganache Icing (page 119)	28 oz / 4 cups

1 Preheat the oven to 325°F. Spray two 8-inch round cake pans with cooking spray and line the bottoms with parchment circles. Lining the bottom with parchment is especially important in this recipe as the chocolate chips often like to stick to the bottom of the pans.

2 In the bowl of a stand mixer fitted with the paddle attachment, cream together the soft butter and sugar on medium-high speed until light and fluffy, 3–4 minutes. On medium speed, add the eggs, one at a time, mixing thoroughly after each addition. Add the mashed bananas and vanilla and mix briefly, just to incorporate. Scrape down the sides of the bowl with a spatula.

3 Add brown rice flour, millet flour, tapioca starch, baking soda, salt, and xanthan gum to the wet ingredients. Mix on medium speed for 2–3 minutes until the mixture is smooth and light. Add the sour cream and whip on high for 1–2 minutes to aerate the batter. Scrape down the sides of the bowl. Add the chocolate chips and stir on low speed just to evenly distribute.

4 Divide the batter between the prepared pans. For 8-inch round cakes, bake for 30–35 minutes, rotating the pans between the upper and lower racks halfway through baking. For 9-inch loaf cakes, bake for 45–50 minutes until a cake tester or toothpick inserted in the center comes out clean.

5 Cool cakes in pans completely and then unmold onto a wire rack before trimming and icing with a thick layer of whipped chocolate ganache, following the method for carrot cake (page 110, step 5).

STRAWBERRY & MERINGUE LAYER CAKE WITH WHIPPED CREAM

This is a true celebration cake consisting of multiple elements and you will need to plan ahead. Make all the components for this cake, except the whipped cream, the day before you plan to assemble it as they should all be cool before you begin assembly. Set aside a few fresh strawberries to use for decorating at the end as well.

The basic vanilla layer cake batter is one you'll want to keep in your toolbox for all sorts of uses. You can transform it into cupcakes, flavor it with lemon or orange zest, or use it as a single layer topped with a fresh citrus or berry compote for a casual dessert. The cake itself is dairy-free and takes on a great flavor from the olive oil. Use a good-quality oil here as you can really taste it in the finished cake.

SERVES 8–10; COOK TIME: (FOR THE CAKE) 40–45 MINUTES; (FOR THE MERINGUES) ABOUT 90 MINUTES; (FOR THE COMPOTE) 5–6 MINUTES

FOR THE CAKE:

Eggs, separated	4 large
White sugar	9.4 oz / 1⅓ cups, divided
Extra-virgin olive oil	7 oz / 1 cup
Unsweetened almond milk	2.6 oz / ⅓ cup
Vanilla paste	1 TB
Brown rice flour	7.3 oz / 1⅓ cups
Millet flour	2.5 oz / ½ cup
Tapioca starch	1.5 oz / ⅓ cup
Blanched almond meal	3.3. oz / 1 cup
Baking powder	1½ tsp
Kosher salt	½ tsp
Xanthan gum	½ tsp

FOR THE MERINGUE:

Egg whites	3 large
Cream of tartar	¼ tsp
White sugar	5.25 oz / ¾ cup

FOR THE STRAWBERRY COMPOTE:

Fresh strawberries, hulled and diced	12 oz / 2 cups
White sugar	3.5 oz / ½ cup
Fresh lemon juice	1 TB

FOR THE WHIPPED CREAM:

Heavy cream	12 oz / 1½ cups
Powdered sugar	2 oz / ½ cup
Vanilla extract	1 TB

1 Make the cake: Preheat the oven to 325°F. Spray two 8-inch round cake pans with cooking spray and line the bottoms with parchment circles. Place the egg whites in the bowl of a stand mixer fitted with the whisk attachment. Place the eggs yolks in a medium mixing bowl and set aside for now.

CONTINUED

2 Whip the egg whites on high speed until they are foamy, 2–3 minutes. Slowly sprinkle in ⅓ cup of the sugar and continue mixing on high speed until the whites form stiff peaks but are still shiny and glossy, not at all dry, 3–4 minutes longer.

3 In the medium mixing bowl, whisk the egg yolks with the remaining 1 cup sugar, olive oil, almond milk, and vanilla paste. Add brown rice flour, millet flour, tapioca starch, almond meal, baking powder, salt, and xanthan gum to the egg yolk mixture and whisk by hand until combined. Switch to a spatula and fold in one third of the beaten egg whites to lighten the batter. You don't have to worry if the whipped egg whites break down a bit at this first addition.

4 Once the first addition of egg whites is well incorporated, add the remaining egg whites all at once. Carefully fold the egg whites into the batter, lifting and folding lightly. You want to lighten the batter without breaking down the whipped whites. The batter should be getting lighter in color and taking on more volume from the addition of the fluffy egg whites.

5 Divide the batter evenly between the prepared pans. Bake for 40–45 minutes, rotating the pans between upper and lower oven racks halfway through baking. Remove from the oven when the cakes feel springy to a gentle touch or a cake tester or tooth-pick inserted into the center comes out clean. Cool completely on a wire rack before assembling or make the cakes a day ahead, wrap in plastic, and refrigerate until ready to assemble.

6 Make the meringues: Preheat the oven to 200°F. Line 2-3 baking sheets with parchment.

7 In the bowl of a stand mixer fitted with the whisk attachment, whisk the egg whites on medium speed until foamy, 2–3 minutes. Add cream of tartar and continue to whisk until the mixture holds soft peaks, another 2 minutes. Slowly sprinkle in the sugar and continue to whisk on high speed until the mixture holds stiff peaks and is thick and glossy, 3–4 minutes. The meringue is ready when you rub a little between your thumb and forefinger and it does not feel gritty, which means the sugar is fully dissolved. If it feels gritty, keep mixing until it feels smooth.

8 Make 3 dollops of meringue, about 4 inches each in diameter, on the prepared baking sheets. Spread each dollop out into an 8-inch disk using the back of a spoon or a small offset spatula to create 3 disks.

9 Bake for about 90 minutes, rotating the pans halfway through baking. Meringues are baked when they are pale in color and crisp to the touch. They should release easily from the parchment paper. Turn off the oven and leave the door propped open slightly to finish drying for several hours or overnight. Meringues can be stored in a zip-top bag for several days at room temperature until you're ready to make and assemble the cake.

10 Make the strawberry compote: Place all the ingredients in a small saucepan over medium heat and bring to a boil. Continue cooking the compote at a full boil, stirring occasionally to prevent sticking, for 5–6 minutes until it has reduced by about half.

11 When the compote is ready, it should be thick and coat the back of a spoon. Take care not to over-reduce here or it will be difficult to spread when cool. Compote can be made up to 2 days ahead and kept in the refrigerator until ready to assemble the cake.

12 Make the whipped cream: Make this just before you assemble the finished cake, on the day you plan to serve it. In a stand mixer fitted with the whisk attachment combine all the ingredients. Whip on high speed until stiff peaks form, about 4 minutes.

13 Assemble the cake: Using a long serrated knife, cut each of your finished cakes in half horizontally. Place one cake layer on a pedestal or serving platter with the cut side facing up. Spread on one third of the strawberry compote, going all the way to the edge. Place one meringue disk over the strawberry spread. Cover the meringue with a thick layer of whipped cream. Repeat the layering process of cake, berries, meringue, and cream two more times. You should now have three layers total.

14 Place the final cake layer on top, with the cut side facing down, so you have a smooth flat surface facing up. Spread the remaining whipped cream on top. Slice a few fresh strawberries in quarters and arrange those in a casual way on the top of the cake.

15 Refrigerate the cake until you're ready to serve. This cake is best served within 2 hours of assembling.

PIES & TARTS

Pistachio Cream Tart with Raspberries

Double-Crust Apple Pie

Almond Frangipane Tart with Apricots

Seasonal Fruit Galette

Buttermilk Pumpkin Pie

Chocolate Bourbon Pecan Pie

Strawberry & Rhubarb Crumble Pie

PISTACHIO CREAM TART WITH RASPBERRIES

There is nothing prettier on a holiday table than this vibrant green and red tart. The filling is delightfully rich, and delicately sweet. Use the freshest, greenest pistachios you can find here as it really makes a difference in both the appearance and flavor of the finished product. Pistachio and raspberry is a classic combination—they balance each other perfectly—but substitute any other nut and jam combination you like. Walnuts and fresh cranberries would be wonderful as would pecans and blackberries. Whatever nuts you choose, make sure you toast them first to bring out all the flavorful oils.

SERVES 8–10; COOK TIME: 45–50 MINUTES

Sweet Pastry Dough (page 224)	12 oz / 1 round of dough
Raw shelled pistachios, toasted	4 oz / 1 cup
White sugar	5.25 oz / ¾ cup
Butter, soft	4 oz / 1 stick
Eggs	1 large
Tapioca starch	1.25 oz / ¼ cup
Heavy cream	1 oz / 2 TB
Grand Marnier	1 oz / 2 TB
Raspberry preserves	6 oz / ½ cup
Fresh raspberries	10 oz / 2 cups
Powdered sugar (optional), for finishing	

1 Preheat the oven to 325°F. Spray a 9-inch tart pan with a removable bottom with cooking spray. Roll pastry dough between two pieces of plastic wrap into a 10-inch disk, ¼ inch thick.

2 Remove the top piece of plastic wrap and, using the bottom piece to help, invert the dough into the prepared tart pan. Gently press the dough down into the pan where the bottom meets the sides. Carefully remove the plastic wrap (now facing up) and use a paring knife to trim the edges of the dough so they're even with the top of the tart pan. Do not leave any overhang. Don't worry if some of your dough breaks off when you invert it. Just patch it back together; no one will ever know.

CONTINUED

3 Line your tart pan with a piece of parchment paper that is large enough to cover the bottom and sides of the pan. Fill the center of the tart with pie weights or dried beans and blind bake the crust for 15 minutes. While the crust is baking, make the pistachio cream.

4 In the bowl of a food processor fitted with the steel blade, process the pistachios and white sugar until a fine meal forms. You're looking for a sand-like texture without any large pieces of nuts. Add the soft butter, eggs, tapioca starch, cream, and Grand Marnier and continue processing until the filling is smooth and creamy.

5 Remove the pie weights and parchment from the baked crust. Spread a ¼-inch-thick layer of raspberry preserves into the bottom of the crust, reaching all the way to the edges. Then spread the pistachio cream over the preserves.

6 Bake the tart for 30–35 minutes until the center is set when pressed gently with your finger. Allow to cool completely. Remove from the pan and place on a cake pedestal or serving platter. Decorate the top with fresh raspberries, in whatever pattern appeals to you. Cover the top completely or leave some of the filling showing, depending on your preference. Dust with powdered sugar, if desired, and serve at room temperature. Tart can be stored, wrapped tightly in plastic, in the refrigerator for up to 2 days.

DOUBLE-CRUST APPLE PIE

My favorite apple for all baking is the Golden Delicious . . . yes, Golden Delicious. They're juicy without being watery. They break down nicely and become perfectly tender without becoming mushy. They have intense apple-y flavor without being too tart. While they might not be my first choice for eating, they are my go-to for baking every time. This is the most classic of all apple pies, with an impressive double crust, and just the thing you want to serve for a special holiday meal. To make life easier, you can top the filling with a Crumble Topping (page 74, step 2), if you prefer, and skip the double-rolling process. Either way you choose, no one will complain when they're served this delicious, homemade beauty of a pie.

SERVES 8; COOK TIME: 60–75 MINUTES

Sweet Pastry Dough (page 224)	24 oz / 2 rounds of dough
Apples, peeled and sliced ¼ inch thick	14 oz / 3½ cups
Brown sugar	2.5 oz / ½ cup
Ground cinnamon	1 tsp
Ground nutmeg	¼ tsp
Kosher salt	½ tsp
Vanilla paste	½ oz / 1 TB
Corn or tapioca starch	1.125 oz / ¼ cup, plus more for crimping
Lemon juice	2 TB, from ½ lemon
Egg yolk	1 large

1 Preheat the oven to 325°F. Spray a 9-inch pie pan with cooking spray. Roll one round of dough between two pieces of plastic wrap into a 10-inch disk, ¼ inch thick.

2 Remove the top piece of plastic wrap and, using the bottom piece of plastic to help lift the dough, invert the dough into the prepared pie pan. Gently press the crust down into the pan where the bottom meets the sides. Carefully remove the plastic wrap (now facing up) and use a paring knife to trim the edges of the dough so they're even with the top of the pie pan.

3 Line your pie pan with parchment paper that is large enough to cover the bottom and sides. Fill the center of the pie with weights or dried beans and blind bake for 15 minutes. While the bottom crust is baking, roll out the top crust following the method described in Step 1; set aside.

4 In a large bowl, toss the apples together with the brown sugar, spices, and salt, vanilla paste, starch, and lemon juice to evenly coat.

CONTINUED

5 Remove the pie weights and parchment from the baked crust. Place the apple filling into the pre-baked pie crust and top with the second round of pie dough that you have pre-rolled. Leave a ¼-inch overhang on the top crust. Fold the edge of the top crust under the bottom crust and crimp using your favorite crimping style to form a decorative edge. If you find your fingers sticking to the dough, dip them in a bit of corn (or tapioca) starch while you crimp. If you don't have a favorite crimping method, use the tines of a fork to connect the top and bottom crusts at the edge of the pie pan and trim off any excess. Cut 3 slits in the center of the crust to allow steam to escape. Brush the entire crust with the egg yolk mixed with 1 tablespoon of water, to help the pie crust brown evenly.

6 Bake the pie for 45 minutes until the top is evenly golden brown and you can see the filling bubbling through the slits in the top crust. It's important to bake the pie until you see it bubbling as that is when the starch will activate and help the filling to properly gel. If the crust is getting too dark during the last stretch of baking, tent with foil and continue cooking until the apples are fully cooked.

7 Allow to cool completely on a wire rack. Serve the same day the pie is made or cover with plastic and allow to rest at room temperature overnight.

ALMOND FRANGIPANE TART WITH APRICOTS

The frangipane in this recipe is intensely almondy and has such a light, creamy quality to it that pairs perfectly with the fresh apricots. Not only is this tart beautiful but I cannot think of a better Mother's Day or Easter brunch dessert. It just screams "Spring!" I make it as soon as I can find good-quality apricots at my local farmers market. In the fall try this tart with poached pears, which is also divine.

SERVES 8–10; COOK TIME: 45–50 MINUTES

Sweet Pastry Dough (page 224)	12 oz / 1 round of dough
Butter, soft	4 oz / 1 stick
Almond paste, soft	3.2 oz / ¼ cup
White sugar	3.5 oz / ½ cup
Eggs	2 large
White rice flour	1.25 oz / ¼ cup
Apricots, halved and pitted	5 medium
Sliced raw almonds	2 oz / ¼ cup
Powdered sugar, for finishing	2 TB
Unsweetened whipped cream (optional), for serving	

1 Preheat the oven to 325°F. Spray a 9-inch tart pan with a removable bottom with cooking spray. Roll pastry dough between two pieces of plastic wrap into a 10-inch disk, ¼ inch thick.

2 Remove the top piece of plastic wrap and using the bottom piece of plastic to help lift the dough, invert the dough into the tart pan. Gently press the crust down into the pan where the bottom meets the sides. Carefully remove the plastic wrap (now facing up) and use a paring knife to trim the edges of the dough so they're even with the top of the tart pan. Do not leave any overhang. Don't worry if some of your dough breaks off when you invert it. Just patch it back together; no one will ever know.

3 Line your tart pan with parchment paper that is large enough to cover the bottom and sides of the pan. Fill the center of the tart with pie weights or dried beans and blind bake the crust for 15 minutes. While the crust is baking, make your filling.

4 In a microwave-safe bowl, place the softened butter and almond paste. Microwave on high power to further soften both to a spreadable consistency, about 90 seconds. In the bowl of a stand mixer fitted with the paddle attachment, mix together the softened butter and almond paste on high speed until smooth, 3–4 minutes.

5 Add the white sugar and mix on medium speed to combine, about 2 minutes. Add eggs, one at a time, mixing until each egg is fully incorporated before adding the next. Finally, add the white rice flour and mix until the filling is smooth and creamy, about 2 minutes more.

6 Remove the parchment and pie weights from the baked tart crust. Pour the filling into the bottom of the crust and smooth with a spatula to form an even layer that reaches to the edges of the pan.

7 Place the apricot halves into the filling in a decorative pattern, with the cut sides facing down. Bake for 40–45 minutes, sprinkling the sliced almonds on top halfway through baking, until the top is golden brown and puffed up around the apricots. The filling may still wiggle when jostled and feel soft to the touch. Don't worry, it will set as it cools.

8 Cool the tart completely on a wire rack. Dust with powdered sugar before serving. Serve on its own or with unsweetened whipped cream.

SEASONAL FRUIT GALETTE

A seasonal galette is rustic elegance that celebrates whatever fruit you choose to fill it with. For the fall and winter holidays, I often choose fresh cranberries mixed with apples or pears—I love the pop of sour flavor and red color they lend to the finished tart. For the summer, any variety of stone fruit is wonderful as is a mixture of berries. You can make this galette vegan by choosing our Sweet Vegan Pastry Dough recipe for equally wonderful results.

SERVES 6–8; COOK TIME: 25–30 MINUTES

Choose from these three fillings:

MIXED BERRIES:

Mixed fresh berries (blueberries, blackberries, raspberries)	12 oz / 2 cups
White sugar	3.5 oz / ½ cup
Ground cinnamon	½ tsp
Cornstarch or tapioca starch	2 TB

STONE FRUITS:

Peaches, apricots, or plums, sliced ½ inch thick	2–3 medium / 2 cups
White sugar	3.5 oz / ½ cup
Lemon zest	1 tsp, from ½ lemon
Vanilla paste or vanilla extract	1 tsp

FALL FRUITS:

Apples or pears, peeled and sliced ½ inch thick	2–3 medium / 2 cups
White sugar	3.5 oz / ½ cup
Fresh cranberries	1.75 oz / ½ cup
Ground cardamom	1 tsp
Lemon juice	1 TB, from ½ lemon

Sweet Pastry Dough (page 224) or All-Purpose Vegan Pastry Dough (page 226)	12 oz / 1 round of dough
Heavy cream or whole coconut milk, for brushing	2 TB
Crystal sugar or coarse AA sugar, for sprinkling	2 TB

1 Preheat the oven to 350°F. Line a baking sheet with parchment.

2 Prepare your fruit filling by tossing together whichever fruit you decide to use with the remaining items in its recipe list. Set aside to macerate for 10–15 minutes while you roll the crust.

3 Roll the sweet pastry dough or vegan dough between two pieces of plastic wrap into a 10-inch disk, ¼ inch thick. Remove the top piece of plastic wrap and, using the bottom piece of plastic to help lift the dough, invert the dough onto the baking sheet. Carefully remove the plastic wrap from the dough.

CONTINUED

4 Place the fruit filling in the center of your disk of dough, leaving a 1½-inch border around the edge. Using a bench scraper or a spatula, lift the sides of the dough in 4-inch sections, folding the dough over the fruit filling and overlapping the dough sections as you go. Don't worry if the crust breaks where it meets the fruit, you can patch and trim it later. I find it easiest to work counterclockwise, starting with the side farthest away from me. Rotate the baking sheet if needed as you go to make the folding easier. The crust should reach over some of the fruit, leaving much of it exposed. If your crust has cracks where it was folded over, gently pinch it back together with your fingers. You want to make sure there are no holes or cracks in the sides of the crust as the juicy filling may leak out and run under the galette, making for a soggy bottom.

5 Brush the exposed crust with heavy cream (or coconut milk if you're making a vegan galette) and sprinkle the entire galette with crystal sugar. Bake for 25–30 minutes (or 30–35 minutes for the vegan pastry) until the crust is golden brown and the fruit is bubbling and tender. Cool completely before serving.

Note: If your fruit has leaked out and run under your galette during baking, you'll want to remove the galette from the parchment after a brief 5-minute cooling period. Otherwise, when the sugar cools your crust will be welded to the paper and difficult to remove. To lift the still-warm galette, use a large spatula (like a pancake flipper) to transfer it from the baking sheet to a wire rack to finish cooling.

BUTTERMILK PUMPKIN PIE

Honestly, pumpkin pie has never been my favorite. However, literally every other person on earth seems to LOVE it! So, I developed this recipe and after many trials, I'm happy to report that I am now a pumpkin pie convert. I love the tanginess of the buttermilk (thanks for the inspo, Martha Stewart!), which makes the filling light and smooth without being overly thick and heavy as many pumpkin pie fillings can be. I also enjoy the sultry blend of spices, which I think is just perfect. We sell hundreds of these pies every Thanksgiving at our shops and I'm always so honored that families order them year after year to share at their holiday tables.

SERVES 8; COOK TIME: 50–60 MINUTES

Sweet Pastry Dough (page 224)	12 oz / 1 round of dough
Pumpkin puree	15 oz / 1 can
Buttermilk	8 oz / 1 cup
Heavy cream	4 oz / ½ cup
Eggs	3 large
Brown sugar	5 oz / 1 cup
Vanilla paste	1 oz / 1 TB
Ground cinnamon	1 TB
Ground ginger	2 tsp
Ground nutmeg	1 tsp
Ground cardamom	1 tsp
Kosher salt	1 tsp
Unsweetened whipped cream, for serving	

1 Preheat the oven to 325°F. Spray a 9-inch pie pan with cooking spray. Roll pastry dough between two pieces of plastic wrap into a 10-inch disk, ¼ inch thick.

2 Remove the top piece of plastic wrap and, using the bottom piece of plastic to help lift the dough, invert the dough into the prepared pie pan. Gently press the crust down into the pan where the bottom meets the sides. Carefully remove the plastic wrap (now facing up) and use a paring knife to trim the edges of the dough so they're even with the top of the pie pan. Crimp the edge of the pie using your favorite crimping design or score with the tines of a fork.

3 Line your pie pan with parchment paper that is large enough to cover the bottom and sides. Fill the center of the pie with weights or dried beans and blind bake for 15 minutes. While the crust is baking, make your filling.

4 In a large bowl, whisk together pumpkin puree, buttermilk, cream, eggs, brown sugar, vanilla paste, ground cinnamon, ginger, nutmeg, and cardamom, and salt until well combined. Pour into the pre-baked pie crust and bake the pie for 35–45 minutes, until done. See note on following page for info on how to tell when a pumpkin pie is baked.

CONTINUED

5 Cool the pie completely on a wire rack. Pie can be served on the same day it was made. Or, store in the refrigerator, wrapped tightly in plastic wrap, for up to 2 days. Serve with unsweetened whipped cream.

How to tell when a pumpkin pie is baked?: Remove it from the oven when it is still jiggly in the center. The filling at the very outer edge and about 2 inches in from the edge should be set and puffed up, maybe with some tiny cracking. Your instincts will tell you, This is not done. Trust me, it's done! If you bake the pie until it looks or feels set in the middle, it will be overbaked and will definitely crack. Why? The pumpkin filling continues cooking the entire time the pie is cooling. So, if it feels done when you remove it, you'll come back later and find fissures in the surface. It's nothing a little whipped cream can't fix. But you've gone to a lot of effort to make a homemade pie and, if possible, you want it to be beautiful when you deliver it to the table.

CHOCOLATE BOURBON PECAN PIE

Chocolate. Bourbon. Pecan. Pie. What's not to love about those four words?! Personally, I often find traditional pecan pie to be a bit too sweet. While this pie is plenty sweet, the bitterness of the dark chocolate balances the sweetness perfectly. It's rich and decadent, and everything you want from a proper pecan pie. This pie easily travels from the Thanksgiving table to a Christmas buffet and everywhere in between. Make sure you make it a day ahead so it has proper time to firm up in the fridge before slicing.

SERVES 8; COOK TIME: 45–50 MINUTES

Sweet Pastry Dough (page 224)	12 oz / 1 round of dough
Bittersweet Chocolate, finely chopped	6 oz / 1 cup
Butter	4 oz / 1 stick
Eggs	8 large
Dark corn syrup	16 oz / 1½ cups
White sugar	14 oz / 2 cups
Kosher salt	½ tsp
Bourbon	2 oz / ¼ cup
Vanilla extract	1 oz / 2 TB
Raw pecan pieces	12 oz / 3 cups, plus 15 pecan halves for decoration
Unsweetened whipped cream or whipped crème fraîche, for serving	1 cup

1 Preheat the oven to 325°F. Spray a 9-inch pie pan with cooking spray. Roll pastry dough between two pieces of plastic wrap into a 10-inch disk, ¼ inch thick.

2 Remove the top piece of plastic wrap and, using the bottom piece of plastic to help lift the dough, invert the dough into the prepared pie pan. Gently press the crust down into the pan where the bottom meets the sides. Carefully remove the plastic wrap (now facing up) and use a paring knife to trim the edges of the dough so they're even with the top of the pie pan. Crimp the edge of the pie using your favorite crimping design or score with the tines of a fork.

3 Line your pie pan with parchment paper that is large enough to cover the bottom and sides. Fill the center of the pie with weights or dried beans and blind bake for 15 minutes. While the crust is baking, make your filling.

4 Place the chocolate and butter in a microwave-safe bowl. Microwave on high power until fully melted, 45 seconds. Whisk to make a smooth emulsion. Set aside while you mix together the remaining filling ingredients.

5 In a large bowl, whisk together eggs, corn syrup, sugar, salt, bourbon, and vanilla until the sugar has dissolved. Stir in pecan pieces. Stir in melted chocolate and butter mixture.

6 Remove the weights and parchment from the baked crust. Pour filling into the pre-baked pie crust and decorate the top with pecan halves as desired. Increase oven temperature to 350°F and bake pie for 35–40 minutes, until the center is still very loose and the sides are very puffy with small cracks. You are looking for an evenly puffed-up surface that resembles a short soufflé, which indicates that the pie is finished. Don't worry, this filling will not set in the oven but it will firm up as it cools.

7 Cool the pie completely on a wire rack then refrigerate overnight. Serve with unsweetened whipped cream or whipped crème fraîche.

STRAWBERRY & RHUBARB CRUMBLE PIE

This pie is my husband's favorite, and his most requested dessert. I make a version of this each summer for his birthday, which occurs at peak season for both fruits. Strawberries and rhubarb are a classic pairing, and for good reason. The sweet jamminess of the strawberries balances the tartness of the rhubarb perfectly. Sprinkle with a brown sugar crumble topping and you have the perfect summer pie. Serve with a scoop of freshly churned vanilla ice cream.

SERVES 8; COOK TIME: 55–60 MINUTES

Sweet Pastry Dough (page 224)	12 oz / 1 round of dough
Fresh strawberries, hulled and quartered	12 oz / 2 cups
Fresh rhubarb, sliced into ½-inch pieces	6.5 oz / 1½ cups
White sugar	7 oz / 1 cup
Vanilla paste	1 oz / 2 TB
Orange juice or orange liqueur	1 oz / 2 TB
Tapioca starch	1.125 oz / ¼ cup
Crumble Topping (page 72, step 2)	10 oz / 1½ cups

1 Preheat the oven to 325°F. Spray a 9-inch pie pan with cooking spray. Roll pastry dough between two pieces of plastic wrap into a 10-inch disk, ¼ inch thick.

2 Remove the top piece of plastic wrap and, using the bottom piece of plastic to help lift the dough, invert the dough into the prepared pie pan. Gently press the crust down into the pan where the bottom meets the sides. Carefully remove the plastic wrap (now facing up) and use a paring knife to trim the edges of the dough so they're even with the top of the pie pan. Crimp the edge of the pie using your favorite crimping design or score with the tines of a fork.

3 Line your pie pan with parchment paper that is large enough to cover the bottom and sides. Fill the center of the pie with weights or dried beans and blind bake for 15 minutes. While the crust is baking, make your filling.

4 In a large bowl, toss together the strawberries, rhubarb, sugar, vanilla paste, orange liqueur, and tapioca starch. Allow to macerate for 10 minutes until juices begin to release.

5 Remove the weights and parchment from the baked crust. Pour the filling into the crust and top with crumble topping. Place the pie on a foil-lined baking sheet to catch any spills, as it tends to bubble up and over while baking. Bake the pie for 40–45 minutes until the filling is bubbling up around the sides and the top is evenly golden brown. It is important to make sure the filling is fully bubbling as the boiling will activate the tapioca starch and will help the filling to properly gel. Cool completely on a wire rack or chill in the refrigerator overnight before serving.

TOASTS

Ricotta Toast for Every Season

Classic Flour Craft Avocado Toast
with Herb Cream Cheese

Avocado Toast with Jalapeño-Cilantro
Hummus & Shaved Vegetables

Avocado Toast with Romesco,
Feta & Toasted Almonds

Banana Toast with Homemade
Chocolate-Hazelnut Spread

RICOTTA TOAST FOR EVERY SEASON

Ricotta toast is one of the most universally loved of all snacks. It's perfect for morning, afternoon, or dessert depending on what you choose to put on top. The key here is finding a really good, flavorful ricotta. Splurge on calories and go for the full-fat option in this case. Look for those made with sheep or Jersey milk if you can find it, for an extra special treat. I can think of a hundred ways to top ricotta toast so use your imagination. If you start with homemade bread like our Country White Sandwich Bread (page 219) or our Buttery Brioche for Loaves (page 213) and excellent ricotta, you really can't go wrong.

MAKES 2 RICOTTA TOASTS PLUS LEFTOVER TOPPINGS; COOK TIME: ABOUT 5 MINUTES FOR TOASTING BREAD PLUS TIME TO PREPARE TOPPINGS

WINTER RICOTTA TOAST

Fresh cranberries	12 oz / 2¼ cups
White sugar	10.5 oz / 1½ cups
Orange zest	1 TB, from 1 orange
Orange juice	4 oz / ⅓ cup, from 1 orange
Lemon zest	2 tsp, from 1 lemon
Country White Sandwich Bread (page 219)	2 slices
Whole milk ricotta	2 oz / ¼ cup
Pistachios, toasted and chopped	1 oz / ¼ cup
Pomegranate molasses	½ oz / 1 TB

1 In a medium saucepan, add the cranberries, sugar, orange zest, orange juice, and lemon zest. Stir until sugar dissolves and cook over medium heat, stirring often, for 8–10 minutes until cranberries pop open and the liquid begins to reduce. Remove from heat and cool to room temperature.

2 Toast bread to desired doneness. Spread ricotta on the toast.

3 Top each ricotta toast with cranberry sauce, sprinkle with toasted pistachios, and drizzle with pomegranate molasses.

SPRING RICOTTA TOAST

Country White Sandwich Bread (page 219)	2 slices
Whole milk ricotta	2 oz / ¼ cup
Ripe kumquats, thinly sliced	5 medium
Coconut flakes, toasted	½ oz / 2 TB
Honey	½ oz / 1 TB
Dried lavender blossoms	1 small pinch

1 Toast bread to desired doneness. Spread ricotta on the toast.

2 Top each ricotta toast with sliced kumquats, toasted coconut flakes, and drizzle with honey. Sprinkle on a tiny amount of dried lavender flowers. A few are delightful, too many and you'll be eating a sachet!

SUMMER RICOTTA TOAST

White sugar	3.5 oz / ½ cup
Water	4 oz / ½ cup
Vanilla paste	½ oz / 1 TB
Ripe apricots, pitted and halved	3 large
Raw almonds, toasted	¾ oz / 2 TB
Country White Sandwich Bread (page 219)	2 slices
Whole milk ricotta	2 oz / ¼ cup

1 Combine sugar, water, and vanilla paste in a small saucepan and cook over low heat until the sugar is dissolved, about 2 minutes. Add apricots and reduce heat to medium-low, gently cooking the apricots until they are tender, about 5 minutes.

2 Remove apricots from the poaching liquid and set aside to cool. Raise the heat to medium and cook until the poaching liquid reduces by two thirds and forms a thick syrup. Set aside to cool.

3 Toast bread to desired doneness. Spread ricotta on the toast.

4 To assemble, top each ricotta toast with cooked and cooled apricots, toasted almonds, and a drizzle of reduced poaching liquid.

FALL RICOTTA TOAST

Ripe Golden Delicious apples, peeled and diced	2 large
Brown sugar	1.37 oz / ¼ cup
Ground cinnamon	1 tsp
Ground nutmeg	¼ tsp
Kosher salt	½ tsp
Maple sugar	½ oz / 1 TB
Hazelnuts, toasted	½ oz / 2 TB
Country White Sandwich Bread (page 219)	2 slices
Whole milk ricotta	2 oz / ¼ cup

1 Preheat the oven to 350°F. Line a baking sheet with parchment. On the baking sheet toss together the peeled and diced apples, brown sugar, cinnamon, nutmeg, and salt. Roast for 20–25 minutes, until apples begin to soften. Set aside to cool.

2 Toast bread to desired doneness. Spread ricotta on the toast.

3 To assemble, top each ricotta toast with cooked and cooled diced apples and sprinkle with maple sugar and toasted hazelnuts.

CLASSIC FLOUR CRAFT AVOCADO TOAST WITH HERB CREAM CHEESE

Avocado toast is the most California of foods but despite the cliché, it really does have all the components you want in a midday snack. This classic version has been the best-selling item at our shops from the day it was introduced. It's really so simple but that's the beauty. Straightforward ingredients combined in the right way can elevate the sum of their parts. I could, and often do, eat this every day. The herb cream cheese is wonderful and makes a tasty spread for any number of other dishes including our Bridgeway Tartine (page 194).

**MAKES 2 AVOCADO TOASTS PLUS
2 CUPS HERB CREAM CHEESE; COOK TIME:
ABOUT 5 MINUTES FOR TOASTING BREAD PLUS
5 MINUTES FOR THE TOPPINGS**

Cream cheese, soft	8 oz / 1 package
Fresh dill, chopped	2 oz / 1 bunch
Lemon juice	1 TB, from 1 lemon
Kosher salt	1 tsp
Ground black pepper	½ tsp
Country White Sandwich Bread, toasted (page 219)	2 slices
Ripe avocado, thinly sliced	½ medium
Flaky sea salt	¼ tsp
Crushed red pepper flakes	1 pinch
Extra-virgin olive oil	1 TB
Microgreens, for sprinkling	

1 Make the herb cream cheese: In a food processor fitted with the steel blade, blend the soft cream cheese, dill, lemon juice, salt, and pepper until well combined. Scrape down the bowl once or twice during blending to make sure there are no lumps in the cream cheese. The mixture should be smooth and creamy, with the herbs evenly incorporated throughout.

2 Spread the herb cream cheese on the toasted bread and top with avocado slices. Sprinkle each toast with flaky sea salt and red pepper flakes. Drizzle with olive oil and sprinkle with microgreens. Serve immediately.

AVOCADO TOAST WITH JALAPEÑO-CILANTRO HUMMUS & SHAVED VEGETABLES

This lovely hummus is also used in our Miller Tartine (page 205). Hummus is one of those ingredients that is worlds better when made at home rather than store-bought, with an ultra-creamy texture you can only achieve when you make it from scratch. Use a good-quality tahini here as its flavor really comes through. I like Soom Foods or MidEast brands if you can find them. You may need to increase or decrease the quantity of lemon juice a bit based on how much oil is in your tahini paste. Just drizzle them into the food processor slowly until the desired consistency is reached. And, when you think your hummus looks creamy and well blended, keep blending it for several more minutes. That extra mixing is the key to ultra-creaminess.

MAKES 2 AVOCADO TOASTS PLUS 2 CUPS HUMMUS; COOK TIME: ABOUT 5 MINUTES FOR TOASTING BREAD PLUS 10 MINUTES FOR THE TOPPINGS

Chickpeas, drained and rinsed	15 oz / 1 can
Tahini paste	4.5 oz / ½ cup
Jalapeño, seeded and deveined	1 small
Fresh cilantro, chopped	1 oz / 4 TB, divided
Ground cumin	2 tsp
Ground coriander	1 tsp
Kosher salt	1 tsp
Ground black pepper	½ tsp
Lemon juice	2 oz / ¼ cup, from 1 lemon
Water	2 oz / ¼ cup
Focaccia with Olive Oil & Salt (page 215), toasted	2 slices
Ripe avocado, thinly sliced	2 oz / 4 TB (½ medium)
Cucumber	1 oz / 2 TB (½ medium)
Radish	1 oz / 2 TB (2 medium)
Carrot	1 oz/ 2 TB (½ large)

1 Make the jalapeño-cilantro hummus: In a food processor fitted with the steel blade, blend the chickpeas, tahini, jalapeño, 3 tablespoons of the cilantro, ground cumin, coriander, salt, pepper, lemon juice, and water until well combined, about 5 minutes. The mixture should be smooth and creamy, with the herbs evenly incorporated throughout.

2 Spread the hummus on the toasted bread. Top with sliced avocado. Using a vegetable peeler or mandoline, shave the vegetables into paper-thin slices and decoratively shingle them on top of the avocado. Garnish with the remaining chopped cilantro.

AVOCADO TOAST WITH ROMESCO, FETA & TOASTED ALMONDS

Romesco—not to be confused with Romanesco—is a wonderful, smoky Spanish spread, which makes a delightful base for this avocado toast. Don't be afraid to make a large batch as it keeps well in the fridge for up to a week and is a great complement to countless other dishes. I love it with eggs and omelettes, or with roasted chicken or fish. It's also a lovely dip for roasted potatoes or cauliflower.

MAKES 2 AVOCADO TOASTS PLUS 2 CUPS ROMESCO; COOK TIME: ABOUT 5 MINUTES FOR TOASTING BREAD PLUS 5 MINUTES FOR THE TOPPINGS

Roasted red peppers, drained	10 oz / 1 jar
Sun-dried tomatoes packed in olive oil, not drained	8 oz / 1 jar
Raw almonds, toasted	5 oz / 1 cup, divided
Smoked paprika	1 TB
Kosher salt	2 tsp
Ground black pepper	1 tsp
Sourdough Bagel (page 165), toasted and cut in half	1 each
Ripe avocado, thinly sliced	2 oz / 4 TB (½ medium)
Feta cheese, drained and crumbled	1 oz / ¼ cup

1 Make the Romesco: In a food processor fitted with the steel blade, blend drained roasted peppers, sun-dried tomatoes with their oil, 3.75 ounces / ¾ cup of the almonds, smoked paprika, salt, and pepper until well combined. The mixture should be creamy with bits of nuts distributed throughout, like a crunchy hummus.

2 Spread the Romesco on the toasted bagel. Top with sliced avocado. Chop the remaining 1.25 ounces / ¼ cup almonds and sprinkle them over the bagel along with the crumbled feta.

Note: All versions of avocado toast are lovely topped with a soft-boiled egg. To make a perfect soft-boiled egg, place however many eggs you'd like to cook in a small saucepan with enough water to cover completely. Bring water to a boil and boil for 5½ minutes. Drain the water and immediately place the cooked eggs into an ice bath. Cool completely and peel. Serve sliced lengthwise on top of the toast so the jammy yolks can ooze onto the bread. Soft-boiled eggs can be peeled and stored in the fridge for up to 3 days.

BANANA TOAST WITH HOMEMADE CHOCOLATE-HAZELNUT SPREAD

If you're looking for the ultimate after-school snack, this is it! Homemade chocolate hazelnut spread is nothing like the overly sweet stuff you buy in the jar that is full of hydrogenated oils and preservatives. This is chunky, chocolatey, and not too sweet. And it actually tastes like hazelnuts! It makes wonderful toast or an excellent topping for Sourdough Pancakes or Waffles (page 43). I'm pretty confident you'll find plenty of ways to use this delicious spread. Eaten right out of the jar is perfectly acceptable as well!

MAKES 2 BANANA TOASTS PLUS 4 CUPS HAZELNUT SPREAD; COOK TIME: ABOUT 10 MINUTES

Hazelnuts, peeled	7.5 oz / 1½ cups
Bittersweet chocolate, roughly chopped	6 oz / 1 cup
Honey (or agave syrup)	1 TB
White sugar	1.75 oz / ¼ cup
Kosher salt	1 TB
Cocoa powder	0.75 oz / ¼ cup
Unsweetened almond milk, warm	2 oz / ¼ cup
Vanilla extract	2 tsp
Buttery Brioche for Loaves (page 213) or Country White Sandwich Bread, toasted (page 219)	2 slices
Ripe banana, sliced	1 medium
Maldon salt (or coarse sea salt)	1 pinch

1 Preheat the oven to 350°F. On a baking sheet, spread out the hazelnuts in an even layer. Toast for about 10 minutes until lightly golden brown and fragrant. Set aside to cool completely. While the nuts are cooling, melt the chocolate and honey together in the microwave on low power, stirring frequently to avoid scorching, until completely melted.

2 In a food processor fitted with the steel blade, blend the toasted nuts, sugar, and salt to form a very fine meal. Add cocoa powder and blend to combine. Add the melted chocolate and honey mixture and blend, scraping down the bowl, until well combined. Drizzle in the warm almond milk and vanilla. The mixture should be thick and smooth. It's ok if bits of nuts remain, they make for great texture. Don't worry if the mixture appears thin. As the chocolate cools, the spread will solidify.

3 Spread the finished chocolate hazelnut spread on toasted bread. Top with sliced banana and sprinkle with flaky sea salt. Extra spread can be stored in the refrigerator for up to 1 week.

SPECIALTY BREADS & PIZZA

Focaccia Pizza Al Taglio

Sourdough Pizza with Pesto, Potatoes & Manchego

Sourdough Bagels

Individual Brioche with Chocolate & Hazelnuts

Hot Cross Buns

Bostock with Almond Frangipane & Fruit

FOCACCIA PIZZA AL TAGLIO

Pizza Al Taglio aka Roman Pizza "by the Slice" is typically rectangular in shape and served by the slice. This pizza uses our basic recipe for Focaccia with Olive Oil & Sea Salt (page 215) and can be topped any way you like. I usually divide the pan of focaccia visually into quarters and top each section differently, then bake it all together. When presented it looks dramatic and can be sliced so each person gets a bit of each of the toppings or gets their very own section. I've made suggestions below for four different toppings but pick what you like and get creative. This is a great recipe to make with your kids as well. The dough is simple enough to make together and each child can create their own section with the toppings of their choice.

SERVES 6–8; COOK TIME: 25–30 MINUTES, PLUS TIME FOR TOPPINGS

Focaccia with Olive Oil & Sea Salt dough (page 215, through Step 3)	1 recipe / half-sheet pan
Toppings (recipes follow)	¼ to 1 recipe (see note above)

1 Preheat the oven to 350°F. Prepare the proofed dough for topping by dimpling the top with your fingers and drizzling with olive oil.

2 Add topping(s) of choice (choose one recipe from the following, or use all four).

3 Bake pizza for 25–30 minutes, rotating the pan halfway through baking.

4 Cool at least 5 minutes before serving. Slice and serve or keep overnight in the refrigerator, tightly wrapped in plastic. Reheat at 350°F for 5–7 minutes the following day.

SUN-DRIED TOMATOES, MOZZARELLA & BASIL

Sun-dried tomatoes, packed in oil	2 oz / ½ cup
Fresh mozzarella, packed in water	3 oz / ½ cup
Fresh basil leaves, finely chopped	1 oz / ¼ cup
Extra-virgin olive oil, for drizzling	
Kosher salt, to taste	

1 Rough chop the sun-dried tomatoes so they form a paste with some pieces of tomatoes still present.

2 Dice the mozzarella into ½-inch pieces.

3 Spread the sun-dried tomatoes evenly over the proofed dough. Sprinkle the top with mozzarella and basil, drizzle with olive oil, and seaon with salt.

4 Bake, slice, and serve according to basic instructions.

ROASTED ZUCCHINI, SQUASH BLOSSOMS & CHÈVRE

Zucchini, thinly sliced	4 oz / 1 medium
Kosher salt and ground black pepper, to taste	
Extra-virgin olive oil, for drizzling	
Squash blossoms	4 large
Soft goat cheese (chèvre)	2 oz / ½ log
Fennel pollen (optional)	1 tsp

1 Preheat the oven to 400°F. Sprinkle zucchini with salt and pepper and drizzle with olive oil. Roast for 15 minutes until zucchini is cooked through and just starting to get crispy around the edges. Allow to cool completely and arrange slices on pizza dough.

2 Remove stamens and stems from squash blossoms. Slice blossoms into strips and sprinkle them over the zucchini. Dot the top of the pizza with chèvre and sprinkle with fennel pollen (if using). Drizzle with olive oil and salt.

3 Bake, slice, and serve according to basic instructions.

CARAMELIZED ONIONS, OLIVES & ANCHOVIES

Yellow onion	1 medium
Extra-virgin olive oil	2 TB, plus more for drizzling
Kalamata olives, drained & pitted	2.5 oz / ½ cup
Anchovies, packed in oil, drained	4 fillets
Fresh basil leaves, thinly sliced	¼ cup

1 Thinly slice onions into half moons. Sauté in 2 tablespoons olive oil on very low heat for 10 minutes until translucent and very soft. They should be caramelized around the edges without burning. Remove from heat and cool completely.

2 Spread the cooled onions over dough. Top with olives, anchovies, and sliced basil. Drizzle with olive oil. Skip the salt here because the olives and anchovies are both plenty salty.

3 Bake, slice, and serve according to basic instructions.

CONTINUED

ROASTED MUSHROOMS, BUTTERNUT SQUASH, RICOTTA & SAGE

Mixed wild or cultivated mushrooms	8 oz
Butternut squash	16 oz / ½ medium
Kosher salt and ground black pepper, to taste	
Extra-virgin olive oil, for drizzling	
Whole milk ricotta	4.5 oz / ½ cup
Fresh sage, thinly sliced	4 leaves

1 Preheat the oven to 400°F. Line a baking sheet with parchment. Cut mushrooms into ½-inch-thick slices. Cut butternut squash into ½-inch dice. Place both on the prepared baking sheet, sprinkle with salt and pepper, and drizzle with olive oil. Roast for 20 minutes or until tender. Cool completely before topping the pizza.

2 Spread cooled mushroom and squash mixture onto pizza dough. Dollop with the ricotta and sprinkle with the fresh sage. Drizzle with olive oil and sprinkle with salt.

3 Bake, slice, and serve according to basic instructions.

SOURDOUGH PIZZA WITH PESTO, POTATOES & MANCHEGO

This sourdough pizza base is yet another great use for the Master Sourdough Starter (page 208). It has excellent flavor and a super-thin, crispy crust. This is a very simple dough but requires a fair amount of resting time, so plan ahead. Start by making the sponge the evening before as it needs to rest overnight. Then mix the dough first thing in the morning, leave it to proof while you're out for the day, and it will be ready for baking by dinner time.

SERVES 4–6; COOK TIME: 40–45 MINUTES, PLUS OVERNIGHT PROOFING

FOR THE OVERNIGHT SPONGE:

Unfed sourdough starter (page 209, through Step 2)	6 oz / 1 cup
Sorghum flour	4 oz / ¾ cup
Water	8 oz / 1 cup

FOR THE SOURDOUGH PIZZA DOUGH:

Brown rice flour	4.2 oz / ¾ cup
Millet flour	3.75 oz / ¾ cup
Tapioca starch	4.5 oz / 1 cup
Golden flaxseed meal	1.25 oz / ⅓ cup
Teff flour	1.5 oz / ¼ cup
Kosher salt	1½ tsp
Brown sugar	1 TB
Xanthan gum	1 tsp
Extra-virgin olive oil	3 TB, plus more for finishing
Warm water	2 TB

FOR ASSEMBLY:

Yukon Gold potatoes	1 pound / 3 large potatoes
Sea salt	2 tsp, plus more for seasoning
Coarsely ground black pepper	1 tsp, plus more for seasoning
Extra-virgin olive oil	1 TB, plus more for drizzling
Manchego cheese	4 oz
Pesto (see recipe following)	4 oz / ½ cup

1 Make the overnight starter: Before feeding your starter for the day, remove 6 ounces for your overnight sponge. Whisk sorghum flour and water into the 6 ounces of starter. Cover and set aside overnight to proof at room temperature.

CONTINUED

2 The next morning, make the pizza dough: In the bowl of a stand mixer fitted with the paddle attachment, mix together brown rice flour, millet flour, tapioca starch, golden flaxseed meal, teff flour, salt, brown sugar, and xanthan gum. Add olive oil, warm water, and the overnight sponge. Mix on high speed for 4 minutes until a smooth, shiny dough forms.

3 Spray a half-sheet pan with cooking spray and put your dough on the pan. Using wet hands, evenly spread the dough all the way to the edges. Drizzle with olive oil and spread the oil evenly across the surface, again using your hands. Cover with plastic wrap and allow to proof in a warm, draft-free place for 4–6 hours.

4 Preheat the oven to 400°F and line a baking sheet with parchment. Slice potatoes ¼ inch thick, leaving the skin on. Put the potato slices on the prepared baking sheet, sprinkle them with salt and pepper, then drizzle with olive oil. Roast for 20 minutes, until tender and the edges are just starting to brown. Set aside to cool completely before using them as a pizza topper.

5 Grate the Manchego using the large holes on a box grater. You should have 1 cup of grated cheese. Spread the pesto on the pizza dough. Top with the roasted potatoes, sprinkle with three fourths of the cheese. Add plenty of freshly grated black pepper, a drizzle of olive oil, and a sprinkling of sea salt.

6 Bake at 400°F for 20–25 minutes, rotating the pan halfway through baking. Sprinkle with the remaining ¼ cup manchego when the pizza comes out of the oven. Allow to cool 5 minutes before slicing.

PESTO

Pesto is best made in the summer when basil is at its peak and it can be frozen for use all year—which is handy because the recipe below makes about 2 cups. Press leftover pesto into ice cube trays and freeze until solid. Unmold them and store in a zip-top bag, and defrost them one at a time for single servings as needed.

Fresh basil leaves	2 oz / 2 cups
Pine nuts, toasted	1.25 oz / ¼ cup
Lemon juice	1 TB
Kosher salt	2 tsp
Ground black pepper	½ tsp
Extra-virgin olive oil	4 oz / ½ cup
Parmesan cheese, grated	1 oz / ¼ cup

1 In the bowl of a food processor fitted with the steel blade, process the basil, toasted pine nuts, and lemon juice together to form a thick paste. Scrape down the sides of bowl with a spatula. Add the salt and pepper and blend. Scrape down the sides again. With the machine running, slowly drizzle in the olive oil until a thick, bright green paste forms. Remove from the machine and stir in the grated parmesan.

SOURDOUGH BAGELS

Most gluten-free bagels are basically just rolls, in bagel shape, which doesn't really cut it in my opinion. A proper bagel should be crusty on the outside, chewy and flavorful on the inside, and these deliver on both fronts. So, my bakers developed this bake-only recipe using a donut pan, a variation of our Sourdough Walnut Loaves (page 210).

MAKES 12 BAGELS; COOK TIME: ABOUT 30 MINUTES, PLUS OVERNIGHT PROOFING

FOR THE LEVAIN:

Unfed Sourdough starter (page 209; through Step 2)	9 oz / 1½ cups
Teff flour	3.5 oz / ¾ cup
Water	6 oz / ¾ cup

FOR THE DOUGH:

Brown rice flour	2.75 oz / ½ cup
Sorghum flour	2.5 oz / ½ cup
Millet flour	2.5 oz / ½ cup
Golden flaxseed meal	2 oz / ½ cup
Tapioca starch	2.25 oz / ½ cup
White rice flour	2.5 oz / ½ cup
Kosher salt	1 tsp
Xanthan gum	1 tsp
Baking powder	1 TB
Brown sugar	1 TB
Olive oil	1 oz / 2 TB
Warm water	8 oz / 1 cup
Cold water, for steaming	16 oz / 2 cups

1 Make the levain: In a small bowl, whisk the sourdough starter with the teff flour and water until evenly combined. Cover and set aside for 1 hour.

2 After about 1 hour, or when levain is bubbly and shows activity, make the dough: In a stand mixer fitted with the paddle attachment, mix the brown rice flour, sorghum flour, millet flour, golden flaxseed meal, tapioca starch, white rice flour, salt, xanthan gum, baking powder, and brown sugar on low speed to combine. Add the olive oil, warm water, and proofed levain. Mix on high speed for 2 minutes until well combined and aerated. The dough should be smooth, shiny, and quite loose.

3 Preheat the oven to 400°F. Place a baking sheet on the bottom rack of the oven. Spray two 6-cavity donut pans with cooking spray. Pipe or spoon in the batter, filling each cavity about seven-eighths full. Place the bagels in the oven. Pour 2 cups cold water onto the preheated baking sheet to create steam and close the oven door quickly. Bake the bagels in the steam for 20 minutes, then reduce the oven temperature to 350°F, carefully remove the steam tray, and bake for another 10 minutes until the bagels are caramel brown on the outside yet still have some give when gently pressed with your finger. Cool in the pans for 5–10 minutes then unmold. Cool completely before serving or store tightly wrapped in plastic on your counter for up to 3 days. Or, place in zip-top bags and keep in your freezer for up to 1 month.

INDIVIDUAL BRIOCHE WITH CHOCOLATE & HAZELNUTS

These delightful little muffin-shaped breads are perfect for breakfast or teatime, a little sweet and a little salty, but not too much of either. Simply paired with coffee and fruit, they're a light breakfast that will be welcomed on any day of the week. Served with my Vegetable Frittata with Herbs & Smoked Trout (page 180), they make a well-rounded celebration brunch. This recipe makes enough for a crowd but they keep perfectly in the freezer for up to 1 month, stored in zip-top bags. Defrost them overnight on the counter and refresh them in the oven for 5 minutes before serving. Simply served with butter and jam, they are as good as freshly baked.

MAKES 24 BRIOCHE; COOK TIME: 20–25 MINUTES, PLUS OVERNIGHT PROOFING

Cornstarch	9.4 oz / 2 cups
Tapioca starch	2.25 oz / ½ cup
Brown rice flour	2.75 oz / ½ cup
Millet flour	1.25 oz / ¼ cup
White sugar	2 TB
Instant yeast	1 TB
Xanthan gum	1 TB
Kosher salt	1½ tsp
Ground cinnamon	1 tsp
Whole milk	10 oz / 1¼ cups
Eggs	3 large
Vanilla extract	2 tsp
Butter, soft, cut into cubes	8 oz / 2 sticks
Bittersweet chocolate, chopped	6 oz / 1 cup
Hazelnuts, toasted & chopped	4 oz / 1 cup
Egg yolk	1 large, for egg wash before baking

1 In the bowl of a stand mixer fitted with the paddle attachment, combine the cornstarch, tapioca starch, brown rice flour, millet flour, sugar, instant yeast, xanthan gum, salt, and cinnamon. Mix on low speed until well combined. Add the milk, eggs, and vanilla and mix on high speed for 3 minutes to aerate the dough. The dough will appear glossy and pale at this stage and will give the resulting brioche a light, airy texture. With the machine running on low add the soft butter, one piece at a time, until all the butter has been added. Turn the machine on high and mix for another 3 minutes to emulsify. The dough should be shiny and sticky. Stir in the chopped chocolate and toasted hazelnuts on low speed.

2 Transfer the dough to an oiled bowl and cover the bowl with plastic wrap. Allow to proof at room temperature for about 2 hours.

CONTINUED

3 Line two 12-cup muffin tins with paper cups. Using a 5-ounce (#6, ⅓-cup) cookie scoop, portion the dough into the muffin cups. Spray the tops of the muffins with cooking spray and cover the pan with plastic wrap. Refrigerate overnight to finish proofing.

4 The next morning, preheat the oven to 325°F. Make an egg wash by whisking together egg yolk and 1 tablespoon of water. Brush the tops of the muffins with egg wash. Bake for 20–25 minutes, rotating the pans halfway through baking. The muffins are done when the tops are light golden brown. Cool in the pans for 5 minutes before unmolding. Serve warm.

HOT CROSS BUNS

Everyone's favorite Easter treat! These are an extremely popular item at our bakeshops every spring. They're an adaptation of our Buttery Brioche Loaves (page 213) with traditional spices and fruits added. They're easy and fun to make with kids on a long holiday weekend. To shape, form loose balls of dough and press them close together in a 9 x 13-inch buttered baking pan. Allow the buns to proof so they grow together and bake up like pull-apart rolls. Don't forget to put an icing cross on each bun, the traditional decoration.

MAKES 12 BUNS; COOK TIME: 20–25 MINUTES, PLUS OVERNIGHT PROOFING

Currants	4 oz / 1 cup
Warm water	4 oz / ½ cup
Cornstarch	9.4 oz / 2 cups
Tapioca starch	2.25 oz / ½ cup
Brown rice flour	2.75 oz / ½ cup
Millet flour	1.25 oz / ¼ cup
White sugar	2 TB
Instant yeast	1 TB
Xanthan gum	1 TB
Kosher salt	1½ tsp
Ground cardamom	1 tsp
Whole milk	10 oz / 1¼ cups
Eggs	3 large
Vanilla extract	2 tsp
Orange zest	1 TB, from 1 orange
Butter, soft, cut into cubes	8 oz / 2 sticks
Egg yolk	1 large, for egg wash before baking
Powdered sugar	4 oz / 1 cup
Orange juice	2 oz, from 1 orange

1 Soak the currants in warm water for 10 minutes while you mix the dough.

2 In the bowl of a stand mixer fitted with the paddle attachment, combine the cornstarch, tapioca starch, brown rice flour, millet flour, white sugar, instant yeast, xanthan gum, salt, and cardamom. Mix together on low speed until well combined. Add the milk, eggs, vanilla, and orange zest and mix on high speed for 3 minutes to aerate the dough. The dough will appear glossy and pale at this stage and will give the resulting buns a light, airy texture. With the machine running on low speed add the soft butter, one piece at a time, until all the butter has been added. Drain the water from the currants and add them to the dough. Turn the machine on high and mix for another 3 minutes to emulsify. The dough should be shiny and sticky.

3 Transfer the dough to an oiled bowl and cover the bowl with plastic. Allow to proof at room temperature for about 2 hours. Once the dough has finished its bulk proofing, and doubled in size, shape it into rolls.

CONTINUED

4 Spray a 9 x 13-inch pan with baking spray. Using wet hands, pick up an orange-sized ball of dough, about ⅓ cup, and toss the ball back and forth between your hands, like you're making a snowball or using a similarly light touch as when shaping a hamburger patty. When formed into a nearly round shape, place the ball of dough into the prepared pan. Proceed until all the dough has been formed. Spray the top of the dough with cooking spray and cover with plastic wrap. Refrigerate overnight to finish proofing.

5 The next morning, preheat the oven to 325°F. Make an egg wash by whisking together egg yolk and 1 tablespoon of water. Brush the top of the buns with egg wash. Bake for 20–25 minutes, rotating the pan halfway through baking. The buns are done when the tops are light golden brown. Cool in the pan completely before unmolding.

6 When the buns are completely cool, mix the glaze. Whisk together the powdered sugar and orange juice until smooth and shiny. Depending on how juicy your orange is, you might not use all the juice. Or, if you find your glaze is too dry, add some water, 1 teaspoon at a time, until the glaze is smooth and thick and no lumps remain. Pipe or spoon the glaze over the buns to form a the distinctive cross design. Allow the glaze to set at room temperature before serving.

BOSTOCK WITH ALMOND FRANGIPANE & FRUIT

Bostock is quite possibly the best-tasting breakfast treat you've never heard of. It tastes like an almond croissant and a fluffy piece of french toast all in one. Thick slices of brioche (page 213) are soaked in lemon syrup, topped with almond cream, sliced fruit, and nuts, and baked into a delicate pastry that is the perfect brunch or teatime treat. Sliced stone fruit like peaches or plums are used here but any berries or berry jam would be equally delicious.

MAKES 6 SLICES; COOK TIME: 10–15 MINUTES

Buttery Brioche for Loaves (page 213)	6 slices, each ½ inch thick
Lemon Drizzle (page 12)	4 oz / ½ cup
Almond Frangipane (page 134, Steps 4 and 5)	6 oz / 1 cup
Sliced stone fruit	3 medium / 2 cups
Sliced raw almonds	3 oz / ½ cup

1 Preheat the oven to 350°F. Line a baking sheet with parchment. Line up the brioche slices on the baking sheet.

2 Using a pastry brush, soak each slice of brioche with 2 tablespoons of lemon drizzle. Spread each slice with 2 tablespoons of almond frangipane. Layer on the sliced stone fruit. Sprinkle with sliced almonds.

3 Bake the bostock for 10–15 minutes until the fruit is soft and the frangipane has melted over the top of the toast and begins to puff and brown. Serve warm.

BRUNCH FARE

Roasted Mushroom, Leek & Gruyère Quiche

Roasted Tomato & White Bean Soup

Vegetable Frittata with Herbs
& Smoked Trout

Stone Fruit, Pistachios & Burrata Salad

Pumpkin, Roasted Squash & Gruyère Strata
with Sage

Cherry Tomato Cobbler

ROASTED MUSHROOM, LEEK & GRUYÈRE QUICHE

Quiche is one of the best anytime meals. Serve with a light green salad for the perfect lunch or brunch. Serve with a side of Roasted Tomato & White Bean Soup (page 179) for a satisfying light dinner. It probably goes without saying that you can use whatever combination of vegetables and cheese you have lying about that you enjoy the most. I love mushrooms, simply roasted at a high temperature, which brings out their earthiness. Make a large batch of the Savory Pastry Dough, defrost when you're ready to make quiche, and you can enjoy a lovely homemade meal quickly and easily.

SERVES 8; COOK TIME: 60–75 MINUTES

Savory Pastry Dough (page 225)	12 oz / 1 round of dough, at room temperature
Leeks, cleaned and thinly sliced	2 large
Cremini mushrooms, thinly sliced	8 oz / 2 cup
Fresh thyme leaves, minced	1 TB, from 2 sprigs
Kosher salt	1 TB, divided
Freshly ground black pepper	2 tsp, divided
Eggs	6 large
Half & half	12 oz / 1½ cups
Gruyère cheese, grated	1 oz / ⅓ cup

1 Preheat the oven to 325°F. Spray a 9-inch quiche pan with a removable bottom with cooking spray.

2 Roll pastry dough between two pieces of plastic wrap to a 10-inch round, ¼ inch thick. Remove the top piece of plastic wrap and, using the bottom piece of plastic wrap, flip the dough upside-down and into the prepared quiche pan. Gently press the crust down into the pan where the bottom meets the sides. Carefully remove the plastic wrap (now facing up) and use a paring knife to trim the edges of the dough so they're even with the top of the pan. Don't worry if some of the dough breaks around the edge. Just use your fingers to press it back into place.

3 Line the dough with parchment paper that is large enough to cover the bottom and sides of the pan. Fill the center with pie weights or dried beans and blind bake the crust for 15 minutes. Remove the weights and set the crust aside while you prepare the fillings. Increase the oven temperature to 375°F.

CONTINUED

4 Place the leeks and mushrooms on a parchment-lined baking sheet. Sprinkle with fresh thyme plus 2 teaspoons of the salt and 1 teaspon of the black pepper. Roast for 20–25 minutes until tender. Leeks should be translucent and mushrooms should have rendered their juices and begun to caramelize.

5 While vegetables are cooking, prepare the custard. In a large bowl, whisk together eggs with the half & half and remaining teaspoon salt and teaspoon pepper until well combined. Set aside.

6 Place the pre-baked quiche crust on a baking sheet. Spread the roasted leeks and mushrooms into the crust and sprinkle the Gruyère over the top. Pour the custard over the vegetables and cheese. Cover with foil and carefully place the baking sheet with the quiche in the oven. Bake for 25–30 minutes. Remove foil and continue baking until quiche is puffed and sides just begin to crack, another 15–20 minutes more. The center should feel set but not completely firm when you remove the quiche from the oven.

7 Cool to room temperature before slicing or wrap tightly with plastic wrap and refrigerate overnight. Quiche is best served at room temperature or ever so slightly warm. If very warm, it may be difficult to slice.

ROASTED TOMATO & WHITE BEAN SOUP

This lovely soup makes a great accompaniment to any of our tartines, toasts, or quiche. It is smoky, nicely acidic, and the addition of the pureed white beans makes it silky smooth yet hearty all at once. In addition to the balsamic vinegar, nice garnish options include thinly sliced basil or toasted focaccia croutons (page 215).

SERVES 4; COOK TIME: ABOUT 20 MINUTES

Yellow onion, diced	1 large
Carrots, peeled and diced	2 medium
Extra-virgin olive oil	2 TB
Fresh rosemary leaves, chopped	from 1 sprig
Cannellini beans, drained and rinsed	1 (15-oz) can
Diced roasted tomatoes	1 (15-oz) can
Kosher salt	2 tsp
Black pepper	½ tsp
Smoked paprika	1 tsp
Crushed red pepper flakes	¼ tsp plus more for serving
Low-sodium vegetable stock (or water)	32 oz / 4 cups
Balsamic vinegar, for serving	

1 In a large 5-quart Dutch oven over medium-high heat, sauté onion and carrot in olive oil until soft, about 3 minutes. Add rosemary and stir until fragrant. Add cannellini beans, roasted tomatoes, salt, pepper, smoked paprika, and red pepper flakes. Sauté for 2 minutes to combine.

2 Add stock and bring to a boil. Reduce heat to a simmer and cook for 15 minutes, stirring occasionally, until liquid has reduced by about one third.

3 Remove from heat and transfer the soup to a blender. Carefully blend, taking care to hold the lid of the blender on tightly when working with hot soup. Puree soup until thick and creamy. Serve garnished with a sprinkling of coarse salt, a pinch of red pepper flakes, and a drizzle of balsamic.

VEGETABLE FRITTATA WITH HERBS & SMOKED TROUT

Frittatas are simple, flexible recipes that can combine any number of ingredients you have on hand. For this version I suggest using seasonal vegetables like zucchini, corn, and cherry tomatoes but, by all means, use what you have. I also suggest including smoked trout, which really elevates this dish. Smoked trout is meaty, sweet, and not nearly as salty or fishy as lox-style smoked salmon. Many good supermarkets stock a wide variety of hot smoked fish in their seafood sections. Look for it there. That said, this is an endlessly flexible and always satisfying dish that should become a staple in your repertoire. A simple frittata really needs nothing more than a light green salad and a cold glass of rosé. Or serve with my Stone Fruit, Pistachio & Burrata Salad (page 185) for something extra special.

SERVES 8–10; COOK TIME: 25–30 MINUTES

Zucchini, sliced into ¼-inch-thick rounds	2 large
Fresh corn kernels, removed from cob	1 cob
Kosher salt	1 TB, divided
Freshly ground black pepper	2 tsp, divided
Extra-virgin olive oil	3 TB, divided
Leeks, white parts only, thinly sliced	1 medium
Cherry tomatoes, halved	5 oz / ½ pint
Smoked trout, skin removed, crumbled in 1-inch pieces	4 oz / ¾ cup
Eggs	12 large
Heavy cream (or whole milk)	2 TB
Sheep's milk feta, crumbled	3 oz / ½ cup
Fresh basil leaves, sliced	2 TB

1 Preheat the oven to 375°F. Line a baking sheet with parchment. Place sliced zucchini and corn kernels in a single layer on the baking sheet and sprinkle with 1 teaspoon salt and 1 teaspoon pepper. Drizzle with 1 tablespoon of the olive oil and roast for about 15 minutes, until zucchini is cooked and corn begins to brown slightly.

2 While the vegetables are roasting, in a large 12-inch nonstick, oven-safe skillet, heat remaining 2 tablespoons olive oil. Sauté leeks over medium heat and sprinkle with the remaining 2 teaspoons salt and 1 teaspoon pepper. Cook, stirring often, until translucent, 3–5 minutes. Remove from heat and add the cherry tomatoes and smoked trout. Stir to combine. Turn the broiler to high once the vegetables have finished roasting.

3 In a large bowl, whisk together the eggs and cream until eggs are light and pale in color. Whisk in the feta and basil and set aside.

CONTINUED

4 Add the roasted vegetables to the sautéed leek mixture and cook for 4–5 minutes over low heat, stirring gently so as not to break up the zucchini too much. Add the egg and cheese mixture to the pan and continue cooking over low heat, pulling the eggs away from the sides of the pan while gently stirring, like scrambled eggs.

5 When the eggs are halfway cooked and there is an even amount of cooked eggs and uncooked eggs in the pan, use your spatula to level out the mixture and place the pan under the broiler. Broil until the frittata is evenly puffed and golden brown and the eggs are fully cooked. Watch the frittata carefully at this stage or it can burn. It needs just 2–3 minutes under the broiler to fully set. Carefully remove from the oven and allow to cool on the stovetop for about 5 minutes.

6 To unmold, run your spatula around the sides of the pan to loosen the frittata. Place a large serving platter or cutting board on top of the pan and invert the pan onto the board or platter. Use caution here because the pan is still hot.

7 Slice the frittata into 8–10 pieces and serve immediately. Frittata keeps well in the refrigerator and is good reheated in the oven or served at room temperature the following day.

STONE FRUIT, PISTACHIO & BURRATA SALAD

This salad is a beautiful assemblage of freshest quality ingredients, highlighting produce when it's at its peak of ripeness. I happen to love yellow nectarines, and their sweet acidity balances the creaminess of the cheese perfectly. But peaches, cherries, plums, or a mixture of them all would be lovely. Serve with fresh mint leaves, loosely scattered over the top of the fruit, and you have a simply perfect summer salad.

SERVES 4; COOK TIME: ABOUT 5 MINUTES

Whole coriander seeds	1 TB
Peaches or nectarines, pitted and sliced into wedges	2 medium
Burrata cheese	8 oz / 1 large ball
Pistachios, toasted and chopped	2 oz / ¼ cup
Fresh mint, roughly torn	2 TB
Fresh basil leaves, roughly torn	2 TB
Maldon salt (or coarse sea salt)	1 TB
Freshly ground black pepper	1 tsp
Extra-virgin olive oil	2 TB

1 In a dry, nonstick skillet, toast the coriander seeds until they become very fragrant and begin to pop. Remove from heat and set aside.

2 Arrange the stone fruit around the edge of a serving platter. Place the ball of burrata in the center of the platter. Sprinkle both the cheese and fruit with pistachios. Sprinkle toasted coriander seeds over the burrata. Sprinkle with mint, basil, Maldon salt, and pepper and drizzle with olive oil.

PUMPKIN, ROASTED SQUASH & GRUYÈRE STRATA WITH SAGE

This recipe gives me all the fall feels and is the perfect thing to tuck into on a chilly fall morning. What exactly is a strata? It's essentially a savory bread pudding. I generally make this with my Country White Sandwich Bread but it would also be wonderful made with my Buttery Brioche for Loaves (page 213), or any other good-quality white bread. Strata is a great make-ahead option to feed a crowd and I couldn't think of anything better for a holiday-morning breakfast. You can make it entirely ahead and just reheat while everyone is busy opening presents. It's a no-fuss crowd-pleaser. Again, this is a flexible recipe. This combination of ingredients is one of my favorites but use what you like and what you have available. Leftover roasted meats and vegetables from Christmas or Thanksgiving dinner would be wonderful here as well.

SERVES 8–10; COOK TIME: 60–75 MINUTES

Butternut squash, cut into ½-inch dice	½ medium / 2 cups
Kosher salt	1 TB, divided
Ground black pepper	2 tsp, divided
Olive oil	2 TB
Eggs	12 large
Whole milk	12 oz / 1½ cups
Heavy cream	12 oz / 1½ cups
Pumpkin puree	1 (15-oz) can
Fresh sage, minced	10–12 leaves
Country White Sandwich Bread (page 219)	1 loaf
Gruyère cheese, grated	4 oz / 1 cup

1 Preheat the oven to 375°F. Line a baking sheet with parchment. Roast the butternut squash with 1 teaspoon salt, 1 teaspoon pepper, and olive oil for 15 minutes, or until tender.

2 While the squash is cooking, prepare the custard. In a large bowl, whisk together eggs, milk, and cream. Add pumpkin puree and whisk until smooth. Add remaining 2 teaspoons salt, 1 teaspoon pepper, and fresh sage. Stir to combine.

3 Cut the loaf of bread into 1-inch cubes. Add the cubed bread to the pumpkin custard mixture and stir to combine. You can push the bread into the custard a bit. You want to make sure the bread has time to absorb as much of the custard as possible before going into the oven.

CONTINUED

4 When the squash is cooked, add it to the bread and custard mixture. Add three fourths of the grated Gruyère and stir to combine. Spray a 9 x 13-inch baking pan with cooking spray. Pour the bread/custard mixture into the baking pan. Press down on the mixture with your spoon to level it out a bit and to make sure the bread doesn't just float on top of the custard. Sprinkle the remaining one fourth of the cheese on top. Cover the strata with parchment paper and then cover the paper with foil, pressing it down firmly around the edge of the pan to seal.

5 Place the baking pan on a baking sheet before putting in the oven, as the strata has a tendency to overflow. Bake, covered, for 35 minutes, remove foil, and bake another 20–25 minutes until the top is golden and the strata is bubbly and feels set when gently pushed in the center. Allow to cool to room temperature before serving.

Note: Strata can be difficult to get cleanly out of the pan. It's best to make this the day before serving and remove it from the pan when it's cold, one piece at a time. You can reheat individual servings on a baking sheet or in the microwave. You will get cleaner-looking pieces when you cut it cold, but whichever way you choose to serve the strata, it will be delicious!

CHERRY TOMATO COBBLER

There is always that point during the late summer when you've eaten your fill of cherry tomatoes but you still have armfuls bursting off the vine. Or, if you don't grow your own garden, they're literally everywhere at the farmers' market, with farmers so eager to offload them they're practically giving them away! That is the time to make this cherry tomato cobbler. You need a LOT of tomatoes and they're really the star of the show here. Topped with a tender biscuit crust, there's not much else you need for a perfect summer meal.

SERVES 6–8; COOK TIME: 45 MINUTES

FOR THE BISCUIT DOUGH:

White rice flour	7.5 oz / 1½ cups, plus more for rolling
Sorghum flour	6.25 oz / 1½ cups
White sugar	3.5 oz / ½ cup
Baking powder	2 TB
Kosher salt	1½ tsp
Ground black pepper	1 tsp
Xanthan gum	1 tsp
Butter, cold	6 oz / 1½ sticks
Eggs	2 large
Buttermilk	10 oz / 1¼ cups, plus 2 TB for baking

FOR THE FILLING:

Cherry tomatoes, mixed varieties	40 oz / 4 pints
Fresh thyme leaves, minced	3 TB
Kosher salt	1 TB
Ground black pepper	1½ tsp
Extra-virgin olive oil	2 TB
Sherry vinegar	1 TB
Tapioca starch	3 TB
Heavy cream, for brushing	2 TB / 1 oz

1 Make the dough: In the bowl of a stand mixer fitted with the paddle attachment, mix together the white rice flour, sorghum flour, sugar, baking powder, salt, pepper, and xanthan gum on low speed for 1 minute, just to combine.

2 Cut the cold butter into 1-inch cubes. Add butter to the dry ingredients and mix on low speed until butter is incorporated and the mixture resembles coarse meal, about 2 minutes more. The butter should be the size of peas.

3 Add the eggs and continue mixing on low speed until just incorporated. Add the buttermilk and continue mixing 2–3 minutes more, until the dough is smooth and comes together in the bowl. Wrap the dough in plastic wrap and refrigerate while you make your filling.

CONTINUED

4 Make the filling: Rinse and pat dry all the cherry tomatoes. Remove any stems. Cut one pint of cherry tomatoes in half. Toss the halved and whole cherry tomatoes with the thyme, salt, pepper, olive oil, and vinegar. Allow to sit for 5 minutes for the tomatoes to release their juices. Sprinkle the tapioca starch over the tomatoes and toss to evenly coat. Transfer the cherry tomatoes to the baking dish while you finish the biscuits.

5 Assemble and bake the cobbler: Preheat the oven to 350°F. Remove the biscuit dough from the refrigerator and dust your counter or cutting board with a light dusting of white rice flour. Using floured hands or a rolling pin, pat or roll dough into a 10-inch round, roughly 1 inch thick. Using a 2-inch biscuit cutter, punch out 10 disks. You can gather your dough scraps and re-roll them just once to punch out 2 more disks, for 12 total. Place the biscuit rounds on top of the tomato filling in the baking pan. Brush the tops of the biscuits with heavy cream.

6 Place the cobbler on a baking sheet and bake, uncovered, for 45 minutes until juices are fully bubbling around the edges and the biscuits are golden brown. Cool before serving. This is best served just slightly warm or at room temperature.

TARTINES & LIGHT LUNCHES

Bridgeway Tartine with Herb Cream Cheese,
Shaved Vegetables & Smoked Salmon

Roasted Beet Salad with Blood Oranges,
Goat Cheese & Walnuts

Stinson Tartine with Brie, Basil
& Slow-Roasted Tomatoes

Yellow Tomato Gazpacho

Creamy Butternut Squash Soup
with Pear & Ginger

Miller Tartine with Hummus, Avocado
& Sun-Dried Tomatoes

BRIDGEWAY TARTINE WITH HERB CREAM CHEESE, SHAVED VEGETABLES & SMOKED SALMON

This simple tartine is a perfect breakfast or lunch for any time of year. It reminds me of a classic European breakfast, which typically leans more savory than sweet. I love using our Sourdough Walnut Loaves (page 210) for this, sliced very thin and layered with many slices of shaved vegetables and curls of smoked salmon. Use a sharp knife or a mandoline to make paper-thin slices of whichever vegetables you like. Sliced cucumber and radishes are my favorites, so that's what I suggest here. And, a bonus recipe is the Dill Cream Cheese, which is a fridge staple at our house and a good spread for almost everything.

MAKES 1 TARTINE, PLUS 2 CUPS CREAM CHEESE; COOK TIME: 5 MINUTES FOR TOASTING BREAD PLUS 10 MINUTES FOR PREP & ASSEMBLY

FOR THE DILL CREAM CHEESE:

Cream cheese, soft	8 oz / 1 package
Lemon juice	2 TB
Fresh dill	4 sprigs
Kosher salt	2 tsp
Ground black pepper	1 tsp

FOR ASSEMBLY:

Dill cream cheese	2 TB
Thinly sliced bread of choice, toasted	2 slices
Radishes, sliced paper-thin	2 large
Cucumber, sliced paper-thin	½ medium
Avocado, thinly sliced	½ large
Smoked salmon	2 oz / ½ small package
Freshly ground black pepper	1 tsp
Microgreens or sprouts	2 TB

1 Make the dill cream cheese: In the bowl of a food processor fitted with the steel blade, process cream cheese and lemon juice until smooth and no lumps remain, 3–4 minutes. Add in the dill, salt, and pepper and continue processing until totally smooth, 1–2 minutes more. Set aside in a sealed container in the refrigerator for up to 1 week.

2 Assemble the tartine: Spread 1 tablespoon dill cream cheese on each slice of toasted bread. Top with alternating pieces of shaved radish and cucumber. Add sliced avocado, smoked salmon, and pepper, and finish with microgreens.

ROASTED BEET SALAD WITH BLOOD ORANGES, GOAT CHEESE & WALNUTS

Think you don't like beets? Try roasting them! Roasting beets brings out the sweetness and eliminates any mushiness you might associate with this underappreciated vegetable. Any variety of beets work well in this salad but my favorites are golden beets or striped chioggia beets, both of which are milder in flavor than red beets.

SERVES 4; COOK TIME: 50–60 MINUTES

Beets, any variety, scrubbed clean	2 pounds / 3–4 medium
Olive oil, for roasting beets	
Dijon mustard	2 TB
Walnut oil (or olive oil)	1.75 oz / ¼ cup
Fresh lemon juice	1 oz / 2 TB
Kosher salt	1 tsp
Ground black pepper	½ tsp
Arugula, roughly torn	1.5 oz / 2 cups, loosely packed
Blood oranges, separated into segments	2 medium
Goat cheese	2 oz / ½ cup
Raw walnuts, toasted	2.5 oz / ⅔ cup

1 Preheat the oven to 400°F. Line a baking sheet with foil. Prick beets with a fork all over, to allow steam to escape while cooking. Rub them with a little oil and wrap each beet tightly in a foil packet. Roast for 50–60 minutes until tender all the way through when pricked with a fork.

2 While beets are cooking, make the dressing. In a large bowl, whisk together Dijon mustard, walnut oil, and lemon juice with salt and pepper until well emulsified. The dressing will taste overseasoned. Don't worry, when mixed with the sweet beets, it will balance out nicely.

3 Open the foil packets and allow the beets to rest until they're cool enough to handle. Gently rub off the skins with a paper towel or clean kitchen towel. They should peel right off. Depending on their size, slice into halves or wedges. Place warm beets in the dressing and toss to coat. As the beets cool, they will soak up the dressing.

4 Arrange arugula on a serving platter and scatter with the oranges, beets, goat cheese, and walnuts.

STINSON TARTINE WITH BRIE, BASIL, & SLOW-ROASTED TOMATOES

This tartine features one of the best flavor-booster ingredients I know: slow-roasted tomatoes. They couldn't be easier but do require some (inactive) time for their low, slow cooking. But, the result is SO worth it! They're little flavor bombs that can be used in all sorts of ways—tossed into salads, stirred into frittatas, used in a salsa for fish or chicken, or featured here in this lovely tartine. Of course they're wonderful made with an abundance of overripe garden tomatoes but you can make them successfully all year. Cooking them this way brings out great flavor even from supermarket tomatoes in the middle of winter. I love this tartine served on our Focaccia with Olive Oil & Sea Salt, which is how we serve it at the bakeshops too.

SERVES 4; COOK TIME: ABOUT 90 MINUTES, INCLUDING SLOW-ROASTING THE TOMATOES

FOR THE SLOW-ROASTED TOMATOES:

Cherry tomatoes	30 oz / 3 pints
Kosher salt	2 tsp
Ground black pepper	½ tsp
Extra-virgin olive oil	2 TB

FOR THE ASSEMBLY:

Focaccia with Olive Oil & Sea Salt (page 215)	2 slices, well toasted
Pesto (page 162)	2 TB
Brie cheese, sliced	1 oz / 2 slices
Roasted tomatoes	1 oz / ¼ cup
Balsamic vinegar	1 tsp
Fresh basil leaves, thinly sliced	2 TB
Extra-virgin olive oil	2 tsp

1 Roast the tomatoes: Preheat the oven to 300°F. Line a baking sheet with parchment. Cut the cherry tomatoes in half horizontally (around their equator). Why horizontally? They tend to hold their shape better when roasted like this. Arrange in a single layer on the prepared baking sheet, with plenty of space between them. Sprinkle with salt, pepper, and olive oil. Roast for about 90 minutes, rotating the pan halfway through baking. When tomatoes are ready, the edges will be dark and caramelized and the center soft and chewy, fairly dry, but still with some moisture.

2 Assemble the tartine: Spread well toasted bread with 1 tablespoon of pesto per slice. Lay on the sliced brie and roasted tomatoes and drizzle with balsamic. Top with sliced basil and a drizzle of your best olive oil and serve!

YELLOW TOMATO GAZPACHO

Think you don't like gazpacho? Well, neither do I . . . except for this one! I have adapted the classic gazpacho recipe to include only the things I like. I prefer yellow tomatoes here if you can find them as they're less acidic and they give the soup a lovely golden hue. Much to my surprise, I've made hundreds of gazpacho converts with this recipe at our bakeshops who have told me this is the only version they'll eat. Feel free to top the soup with golden focaccia croutons (page 215) for a perfect cooling summer meal. I hope you'll also love it and make some new converts of your own.

SERVES 4; COOK TIME: 10 MINUTES, PLUS CHILLING

Yellow tomatoes, roughly chopped	4 large (1½–2 pounds)
English cucumber, roughly chopped	1 large
Fresh basil, torn	4 sprigs, or to taste
Scallion, roughly chopped	2 medium
Corn kernels, fresh or frozen	1 cup
Slivered blanched almonds	¾ cup
Thai red chile pepper	1 medium
Sherry vinegar	2 TB
Smoked paprika	1 tsp
Kosher salt	1 TB, plus more to taste
Ground black pepper	1 tsp, plus more to taste
Extra-virgin olive oil	2 TB, plus more for drizzling
Cold water	2–3 cups
Sliced cherry tomatoes, for garnish	2 TB
Chopped raw almonds, for garnish	2 TB
Chopped fresh chives, for garnish	1 TB

1 Put all the ingredients except garnishes and including 2 cups of the water, in the jar of a blender and process until smooth. Add additional water up to 1 cup as needed to achieve a smooth and pourable consistency. If additional water will not fit in the blender jar, you can process the gazpacho until the mixture is thick like a smoothie and whisk in additional water after it's poured into a bowl.

2 Pour the processed soup into a large bowl. Season to taste with salt and pepper. Chill for at least 2 hours before serving. Garnish with sliced cherry tomatoes, chopped almonds, and chives.

CREAMY BUTTERNUT SQUASH SOUP WITH PEAR & GINGER

This is by far and away the most popular soup I have ever made for our bakeshops. It's everything you want on a chilly fall day and it just so happens to be dairy-free as well. It's smooth, creamy, and very satisfying. It's perfect served alongside a few slices of toasted focaccia (page 215) or with our Mushroom, Leek & Gruyère Quiche (page 176). I'd suggest you put it in your cold weather rotation. It needs nothing more than a quick drizzle with extra coconut milk and a few grinds of black pepper for a simple lunch, sure to be loved by everyone.

SERVES 4; COOK TIME: 40–45 MINUTES

Butternut squash, cut into 1-inch dice	2 pounds / 1 large
Leeks, sliced, white & light green parts only	2 medium
Anjou or Bartlett pears, cored and diced	2 large
Kosher salt	1 TB, plus more to taste
Ground black pepper	1 tsp, plus more to taste
Extra-virgin olive oil	2 TB
Fresh ginger, peeled and minced	1-inch piece
Low-sodium vegetable stock (or water)	48 oz / 6 cups
Coconut milk (preferably light)	1 (15-oz) can

1 Preheat the oven to 375°F. Line a baking sheet with parchment. Arrange squash, leeks, and pears on the baking sheet. Sprinkle with salt, pepper, and olive oil and roast for 30 minutes until the vegetables and fruit are fairly tender. Don't worry if they're not all the way cooked through as they'll finish cooking on the stovetop.

2 Transfer roasted vegetables to a large (5-quart) Dutch oven or stockpot. Add the chopped fresh ginger. Cover with stock and bring to a boil. Reduce to a simmer and cook for 10–15 minutes, until vegetables are tender and the flavors come together.

3 Working in batches, carefully transfer soup to a blender and puree until very smooth, taking care to cover the blender and hold the lid on tightly when working with hot soup. Return the pureed soup to the stockpot and whisk in the coconut milk. Season to taste with salt and pepper. If the soup seems too thick, add a bit more water until it reaches desired consistency.

MILLER TARTINE WITH HUMMUS, AVOCADO & SUN-DRIED TOMATOES

The hummus in this recipe is reason enough to try this tartine. Making your own hummus is really quick and easy and worlds better than even the best hummus you can buy at the store. The key to making excellent hummus is to process it to oblivion. When you think it's creamy enough, keep going, and process it for several minutes more. This extra time is sure to give you the creamiest, dreamiest hummus you've ever had. Keep the hummus in your fridge for dipping, serving with falafel, or spreading liberally on this delicious tartine. Served with a hearty salad like my Roasted Beet Salad with Blood Oranges, Goat Cheese & Walnuts (page 197), it's also substantial enough for dinner or perfect for a picnic.

MAKES 2 TARTINES; COOK TIME: 5 MINUTES FOR TOASTING BREAD PLUS 10 MINUTES FOR PREP & ASSEMBLY

Focaccia with Olive Oil & Sea Salt (page 215), well toasted	2 slices
Jalapeño-Cilantro Hummus (page 152)	3 oz / ½ cup
Sun-dried tomatoes packed in oil, chopped	1 oz / 2 each
Hard-boiled egg, sliced	1 large
Avocado, sliced	½ large
Microgreens or baby arugula	2 TB

1 Spread each slice of well-toasted focaccia with the freshly made hummus.

2 Top the tartines with sun-dried tomatoes, sliced egg, avocado, and microgreens, dividing the ingredients equally. Serve immediately.

MASTER RECIPES

Sourdough Starter

Sourdough Walnut Loaves

Buttery Brioche for Loaves

Focaccia with Olive Oil & Salt

Country White Sandwich Bread

Sweet Scones

Savory Scones

Sweet Pastry Dough

Savory Pastry Dough

All-Purpose Vegan Pastry Dough

SOURDOUGH STARTER

At the heart of all the sourdough recipes in this book is this sourdough starter. Sourdough starter is a labor of love, as it needs to be tended and fed like any living thing. It's really nothing more than flour and water mixed together that, when allowed to absorb the bacteria present in the air, grows into a living, breathing thing. Developing a starter takes anywhere from 5–20 days for fermentation to begin. Be patient with this process. You may go through a few iterations before your starter takes. A minimal amount of ingredients is involved, so just try again. The amount of time needed depends on the temperature in your house, the moisture in the air, and how much "wild" bacteria is present. If it's cold outside and your windows and doors are closed, there may be less bacteria to work with. If it's warmer and your house is more open, there will be more wild bacteria present and the starter will usually develop faster.

Each sourdough starter is unique and depends on the particular bacteria culture in your environment, the temperature and humidity present in your space, the pH of your particular water, and more. Our bakery's starter, which we named "Matilda," changes character throughout the year as those factors vary in our environment as well. Since we feed her daily and care for her like a precious member of the family, we thought she deserved a name. Your sourdough starter will take on a life of its own as well. While a home starter really only needs to be fed once a week once developed, it is something that does need constant attention, so you should be committed to baking bread or making waffles at least once a week so you can use it.

My gluten-free flour of choice for sourdough is teff flour. Teff is the smallest grain in the world and native to northern Africa. If you've ever eaten injera in an Ethiopian restaurant, you've enjoyed teff flour. It is highly fermentable and has a pleasantly sour, yogurt-like flavor and reddish-brown color, both of which I find very appealing. Surprisingly, these days teff is available at most well-stocked natural markets, but if you can't find teff, my next favorite option for sourdough is white sorghum flour.

If you do use sorghum flour, your end result will be lighter in color and have a slightly sharper sour flavor. I've also found that it's less visibly active. There will be bubbles on the surface of your starter but they will be smaller and less bubbly than the highly active teff.

MAKES 1 QUART STARTER; TIME: 2 MINUTES, PLUS 5–20 DAYS TO DEVELOP THE STARTER

Teff flour (or sorghum flour)	1.375 oz / ¼ cup
Filtered water, room temp	2 oz / ¼ cup

1 In a large, wide-mouthed glass jar with plenty of room to spare, whisk together the teff flour and water. Allow to rest, uncovered on an open windowsill or in a well-ventilated room for at least 5 days, or up to 3 weeks.

2 After a few days or maybe a week or so, you will start to see bubbles form on the surface of the starter. Be patient. It can take longer than you'd expect for this to happen. Just leave it alone and check in on it every couple of days. Once you see active bubbles (think beer), that is the time to start feeding it. To feed, whisk in 2 tablespoons flour and 2 tablespoons water every other day or so. After you feed your starter for the first time, allow it to rest on the counter for 4–6 hours, until you see bubbles form on the surface of the starter. Once bubbles appear, cover and store the starter in the refrigerator for up to 1 week before feeding again.

3 Continue this process for 3–5 more days, until your starter has developed a pleasantly sour flavor/aroma and is very active after feeding. Your starter will be quite large at this point and you will have enough volume to use in any of the sourdough recipes that follow. The sourdough recipes in this book call for "unfed" starter. This simply means the portion removed from the original starter for a recipe should not be fed ahead of use in that recipe. After removing enough starter for whichever recipe you choose, feed it, and place the remaining starter in the refrigerator to rest until you need it again.

4 Remember, every time you use your starter you must feed it by replacing what you took out. For example, if you take out 1 cup of starter for a recipe, you will need to replace it by feeding it with ½ cup flour plus ½ cup water. And, never let your starter get down to less than one fourth of the base volume. If you take out all of your starter and/or wash the vessel in which it lives, you will need to start the whole process over from Step 1.

SOURDOUGH WALNUT LOAVES

This recipe is the one to date that has taken me the longest to get just right. In the end, though, all the months of effort were well worth it. I literally eat this bread every single day. I even pack it in my suitcase when I travel so I can have my proper morning toast. Yes, I actually do that! It has a great crusty exterior and a moist, sour interior that has the exact doughiness you'd expect from a good loaf of true sourdough. This dough also makes lovely bagels, just as is, piped into a donut or bagel pan. I generally add walnuts to this dough as indicated in the recipe—I love the crunch they give to the interior and the look they give to the finished loaf. But this bread is also delicious on its own, or add the nut or seed of your choice. Hazelnuts or hemp, pumpkin, or sunflower seeds would all be good choices.

MAKES TWO 9-INCH LOAVES; COOK TIME: 60–65 MINUTES, PLUS OVERNIGHT PROOFING

FOR THE LEVAIN:

Sourdough starter, unfed (page 209; through Step 2)	17 oz / 2 cups
Teff flour	5.5 oz / 1 cup
Cool water	12 oz / 1½ cups

FOR THE DOUGH:

Brown rice flour	5.5 oz / 1 cup
Sorghum flour	5 oz / 1 cup
Millet flour	5 oz / 1 cup
Golden flaxseed meal	4 oz / 1 cup
Tapioca starch	4.5 oz / 1 cup
White rice flour	5 oz / 1 cup
Kosher salt	2 tsp
Xanthan gum	2 tsp
Baking powder	2 TB
Brown sugar	2 TB
Olive oil	2 oz / ¼ cup
Warm water	16 oz / 2 cups
Raw walnuts (optional)	4.5 oz / 1 cup
Unsweetened almond milk, for brushing	2 TB

1 Mix the levain: Remove 2 cups of unfed starter for the levain. In a small bowl, whisk teff flour and water together with the starter until smooth. Set aside for at least 30 minutes and up to 2 hours while you mix the dough.

2 Make the dough: In a stand mixer fitted with the paddle attachment, combine brown rice flour, sorghum flour, millet flour, golden flaxseed meal, tapioca starch, white rice flour, salt, xanthan gum, baking powder, and brown sugar. Mix on low speed for 1 minute, just to combine. Add the olive oil, warm water, and levain mixture and mix on high speed for 2 minutes until the dough is smooth and light in color. Add the walnuts (if using) and mix on low speed for 30 seconds more to combine.

3 Spray two 9 x 5-inch loaf pans with non-stick cooking spray. Using wet hands, divide the dough evenly between the pans, taking care not to press down on the dough too much. It should be peaky and fluffy when placed into the pans. Spray the top of the loaves with cooking spray and cover them with plastic wrap. Allow to rest overnight at room temperature. The loaves should rise to the top of the bread pans.

4 Preheat the oven to 425°F. Place a dry, empty baking sheet in the bottom of the oven. Fill a 1-cup liquid measure with tap water. You will use this to create steam. Remove the plastic wrap from the loaves and brush the tops with almond milk. Place loaves in the preheated oven on the middle rack. Pour the reserved water onto the preheated baking pan to create steam. Quickly close the oven door and bake the loaves (with steam) for 20 minutes. Reduce the oven temperature to 375°F and continue baking for 40–45 minutes longer, until the loaves are a deep golden brown and have formed a nice crust on the top. Remove the loaves from their pans immediately and cool completely on a wire rack. Loaves will keep, wrapped well in plastic, on the counter for up to 5 days, or slice and freeze for up to 1 month. Frozen slices can go straight into the toaster.

BUTTERY BRIOCHE FOR LOAVES

Brioche is the queen of enriched dough. It's filled with butter, eggs, and milk for a bread that's absolutely divine for life in general but also for French toast and grilled cheese sandwiches, as well as pastries like Individual Brioche with Chocolate & Hazelnuts (page 166) or Bostock (page 172). Brioche is quite easy to make and perfumes the whole house with a fabulous buttery aroma as it bakes. Be advised that this dough benefits from an overnight proof in the refrigerator before baking, so mix and rest it the day before you need it. The finished bread also keeps well stored in the freezer for up to 1 month so you can have it on demand anytime you fancy a perfect slice of buttered toast.

MAKES TWO 9-INCH LOAVES; COOK TIME: ABOUT 45 MINUTES, PLUS OVERNIGHT PROOFING

Cornstarch	18.8 oz / 4 cups
Tapioca starch	4.5 oz / 1 cup
Brown rice flour	5.5 oz / 1 cup
Millet flour	2.5 oz / ½ cup
White sugar	1.75 oz / ¼ cup
Instant yeast	2 TB
Xanthan gum	2 TB
Kosher salt	1 TB
Whole milk	20 oz / 2½ cups
Eggs	5 large
Vanilla extract	½ oz / 1 TB
Butter, soft, cut into cubes	16 oz / 4 sticks
Egg yolk, for egg wash	1 large

1 In the bowl of a stand mixer fitted with the paddle attachment, combine cornstarch, tapioca starch, brown rice flour, millet flour, sugar, instant yeast, xanthan gum, and salt. Mix together on low speed until well mixed, 1–2 minutes. Add the milk, eggs, and vanilla and mix on high speed for 3 minutes to aerate the dough. With the machine running on low, add the soft butter, one piece at a time, until all the butter has been added. Turn the machine on high and mix for another 3 minutes to emulsify. The dough will be shiny and sticky.

CONTINUED

2 Transfer the dough to an oiled bowl and cover with plastic wrap. Allow to proof at room temperature for about 2 hours. Once the dough has finished its bulk proofing and has doubled in size, you can shape it into loaves.

3 Spray two 9 x 5-inch loaf pans with cooking spray. Using wet hands, transfer the dough to the prepared pans and shape the loaves, pressing into the corners to form a rounded top and tapered sides. Spray the top of the loaves with cooking spray and cover them with plastic wrap. Refrigerate overnight to finish proofing.

4 The next morning, preheat the oven to 350°F. Make an egg wash by whisking the egg yolk with 1 tablespoon of water. Brush the tops of the loaves with the egg wash. Bake for 45 minutes, rotating the pans between the upper and lower oven racks halfway through baking. Tops should be light golden brown and the loaves intensely fragrant. Cool the loaves in the pans for 5 minutes, then unmold and let them finish cooling on a wire rack before slicing.

FOCACCIA WITH OLIVE OIL & SEA SALT

This has been our best-selling bread at the bakeshops since day one. It's super versatile and universally loved by adults and kids alike. Its crumb is delicate and tender and, like every proper focaccia, it's moist with good olive oil and topped with crunchy sea salt. At the shops we slice it horizontally and use it for sandwiches. Or, toast it on the stovetop with just a touch of olive oil until golden for crispy croutons to make panzanella or as a crunchy topping for soup. You can also grind it for breadcrumbs (which are the world's best coating for anything breaded and fried), top it like pizza . . . the options are many! The recipe below is for our basic focaccia and is the perfect base for any of the above ideas.

SERVES 6–8; COOK TIME: 25–30 MINUTES, PLUS OVERNIGHT PROOFING

Brown rice flour	5.5 oz / 1 cup
Millet flour	5 oz / 1 cup
Tapioca starch	16.87 oz / 3¾ cups
Brown sugar	2.5 oz / ½ cup
Instant yeast	2 TB
Baking powder	2 TB
Xanthan gum	1½ tsp
Fruit pectin	1 TB
Kosher salt	1½ tsp
Warm water	20 oz / 2½ cups
Extra-virgin olive oil	4 oz / ½ cup, plus more for drizzling
Egg whites	4 oz / 4 large
Apple cider vinegar	1 tsp
Maldon salt (or coarse sea salt)	1 TB

1 Spray a half-sheet pan with cooking spray. In the bowl of a stand mixer fitted with the paddle attachment, combine brown rice flour, millet flour, tapioca starch, brown sugar, instant yeast, baking powder, xanthan gum, fruit pectin, and salt. Mix on low speed for 1 minute. Add water, ½ cup olive oil, egg whites, and vinegar and mix on high speed for 5 minutes, until the dough is smooth and shiny.

2 Transfer the dough to your prepared half-sheet pan. Using wet hands, pat the dough out so it evenly covers the sheet pan and reaches all the way into the corners. Drizzle 1–2 tablespoons of olive oil over the top and use your hands to spread the oil evenly over the surface of the dough.

3 Cover the dough with plastic wrap and allow to proof at room temperature for 20 minutes, then refrigerate overnight.

CONTINUED

4 When ready to bake, preheat the oven to 350°F. Drizzle 1–2 tablespoons more olive oil over the top and, using your fingers, gently "dimple" the dough. Poke straight down with your fingers rather than dragging or pulling your fingers through the dough. Your dimples should reach about halfway through the dough. Sprinkle the top with Maldon salt.

5 Bake for 25–30 minutes, rotating the pan halfway through baking, until the bread is evenly golden brown with a crispy top. Allow the focaccia to cool before slicing. Extra bread can be frozen for up to 1 month or wrapped in plastic wrap and stored at room temperature for up to 4 days. Re-toast before serving.

VARIATIONS

Festive Fruit: Add candied and dried fruits for a festive holiday bread. The sweetness of the fruit and the saltiness of the focaccia makes for a truly addictive treat. After the wet ingredients have been added, mix in 1 cup of your favorite fruits during the last minute of mixing. I like dried cranberries, candied orange peel, and candied lemon peel. Follow the same proofing and baking instructions.

Olive & Herb: Add olives and dried herbs to your focaccia for a wonderful savory addition. After the wet ingredients have been added, mix in 1 cup of halved kalamata olives and 2 tablespoons herbs de provence during the last 1 minute of mixing. Follow the same proofing and baking instructions.

Sharp Cheddar & Black Pepper: Add sharp cheddar and black pepper to your basic dough for a spicy and savory treat. After the wet ingredients have been added, mix in 1 cup grated cheddar cheese and 1 tablespoon coarsely ground black pepper during the last 1 minute of mixing. Follow the same proofing and baking instructions.

COUNTRY WHITE SANDWICH BREAD

This is a customer favorite at our bakeries. It's universally loved by children and adults alike. It has a light interior, crusty golden exterior, and a soft texture. It can be sliced thin for sandwiches or toast, keeps well on the counter for several days, and toasts up great on demand. I generally top these loaves with sesame seeds as they add a nice visual finish to the bread.

MAKES ONE 9-INCH LOAF; COOK TIME: 50–60 MINUTES, PLUS 10–15 MINUTES PROOFING

Brown rice flour	2.75 oz / ½ cup
Corn flour	2 oz / ⅓ cup
Millet flour	1.25 oz / ¼ cup
Tapioca starch	9 oz / 2 cups
Brown sugar	1.375 oz / ¼ cup
Instant yeast	1 TB
Baking powder	1 TB
Xanthan gum	2 tsp
Fruit pectin	1½ tsp
Kosher salt	1 tsp
Warm water	10 oz / 1¼ cups
Olive oil	1.75 oz / ¼ cup
Egg whites	2 oz / 2 large
Apple cider vinegar	½ tsp
Egg yolk, for egg wash	1 large
Sesame seeds	1 TB

1 Preheat the oven to 350°F. In the bowl of a stand mixer fitted with the paddle attachment, combine brown rice flour, corn flour, millet flour, tapioca starch, brown sugar, instant yeast, baking powder, xanthan gum, fruit pectin, and salt. Mix on low speed to combine, 1–2 minutes.

2 Add the warm water, olive oil, egg whites, and vinegar and mix on high speed for 3–4 minutes, until the dough is light in color and well aerated. The dough will be shiny and smooth and the aeration will result in a lighter, fluffier finished loaf.

3 Spray a 9 x 5-inch loaf pan with nonstick cooking spray. Place the dough in the pan and, using wet hands, smooth the dough into an even, rounded loaf shape. Make an egg wash by whisking the egg yolk with 1 tablespoon of water. Brush the egg wash onto the loaf and sprinkle with sesame seeds.

4 Set your loaf aside to proof for 10–15 minutes. Depending on the temperature in the room, proofing may take more or less time. Proofed loaves should have risen considerably, above the sides of the pan, and be neatly domed in the middle before baking.

5 Bake the loaf for 50–60 minutes, rotating the pan halfway through baking, until the top is very puffed and is a warm, golden color. Remove the loaf from the pan while it's hot and allow it to cool completely on a wire rack before slicing.

SWEET SCONES

This recipe should be a go-to for every home baker. It's endlessly adaptable and very flexible. Put your unique spin on this basic dough or try one of the adaptations in this book, like Raspberry & Almond Scones (page 26). The scone dough can be made well ahead and baked straight from frozen when you're ready to serve. Scones have been top-selling items at our bakeshops since day one. People love our scones—they're rich and satisfying yet not too sweet, and they're perfect any time of day with a warm drink. A few of my favorite flavor combinations are: blueberry-lemon, blackberry–Earl Grey, apple-spice, chocolate-ginger, and cranberry-orange.

MAKES 24 SCONES; COOK TIME: 23–28 MINUTES

Brown rice flour	16.5 oz / 3 cups, plus more for dusting
White sugar	5 oz / ¾ cup
Baking powder	1 TB plus 1 tsp
Kosher salt	1 tsp
Xanthan gum	1 tsp
Cold butter, cut into 1-inch cubes	6 oz / 1½ sticks
Eggs	2 large
Heavy cream	10 oz / 1¼ cups, plus 2 TB for baking
Mix-Ins of your choice (see note above)	1–2 cups
Coarse sugar or crystal sugar	2 TB for baking

1 In the bowl of a stand mixer fitted with the paddle attachment, mix together brown rice flour, sugar, baking powder, salt, and xanthan gum on low speed to combine, 1–2 minutes.

2 Cut the cold butter into 1-inch cubes. Add the butter to the dry ingredients and mix on low speed until the butter is incorporated and the mixture resembles coarse meal, 2–3 minutes more. The butter should be the size of peas.

3 Add the eggs and continue mixing until just incorporated, 1–2 minutes. Add the heavy cream and mix on low speed until the dough is smooth and comes together in the bowl, another 2 minutes or so.

4 Add the mix-ins. Mix very briefly, just to combine. You want the additions to remain intact.

5 Divide the dough into three equal-sized balls and wrap each tightly in plastic wrap. Refrigerate at least 30 minutes, or up to overnight. .

6 Preheat the oven to 375°F. To shape the scones, flour your counter or cutting board with a light dusting of brown rice flour. Using floured hands, pat the chilled dough ball into an 8-inch disk, roughly 1 inch thick. Using a sharp knife or a bench scraper, form the scones. Cut the dough disk in half, then cut each half in half (you now have 4 quarters), then cut each quarter in half yet again to form 8 wedges per round. At this point, you can also freeze the unbaked scones in zip-top bags for up to 1 month. Bake them straight from the freezer, using the baking time and temperature in the recipe.

7 Place the scones on two parchment-lined baking sheets, spaced about 2 inches apart. Brush the scones with the remaining 2 table-spoons heavy cream, and dust them with a sprinkling of coarse sugar. Bake for 18 minutes. Rotate the pans and bake for another 8–10 minutes, until the scones are lightly brown on the top and feel just set to the touch. Allow to cool for 10 minutes on the baking sheet before removing. Fresh scones are best served warm on the day they are made or freeze cooled scones in a zip-top bag for up to 1 month.

SAVORY SCONES

Savory scones are similar to biscuits but more cakey and less flaky. They're a special treat when served alongside a homemade soup for a cozy dinner. They also make a lovely accompaniment to any egg dish at the brunch table. Adapt this any number of ways but, as a general rule, including a cheese, an herb, and something salty or crunchy like a toasted nut is a good place to start. A few suggestions for flavor combinations are: Roasted Pears, Blue Cheese & Toasted Walnuts (page 53); cheddar and chive; goat cheese and sun-dried tomatoes with basil; Gruyère and rosemary; or Marcona almond and fig with Gorgonzola.

MAKES 24 SCONES; COOK TIME: 23–28 MINUTES

Brown rice flour	16.5 oz / 3 cups plus more for dusting
White sugar	1.75 oz / ¼ cup
Baking powder	1 TB plus 1 tsp
Kosher salt	1 tsp
Xanthan gum	1 tsp
Cold butter, cut into 1-inch cubes	6 oz / 1½ sticks
Eggs	2 large
Heavy cream	10 oz / 1¼ cups, plus 2 TB for baking
Toasted nuts	2 oz / ½ cup, plus more for topping scones
Fresh herbs, chopped	2 TB
Grated or crumbled cheese	3 oz / ½ cup
Coarse sea salt	1 TB, for baking
Ground black pepper	1 tsp

1 In the bowl of a stand mixer fitted with the paddle attachment, mix together brown rice flour, sugar, baking powder, salt, and xanthan gum on low speed to combine, 1–2 minutes.

2 Cut the cold butter into 1-inch cubes. Add the butter to dry ingredients and mix on low speed until the butter is incorporated and the mixture resembles coarse meal, 2–3 minutes more. The butter should be the size of peas.

3 Add the eggs and mix until just incorporated, 1–2 minutes. Add the heavy cream and mix on low speed until the dough is smooth, about 2 minutes more.

4 Add the mix-ins. Mix on low speed very briefly for 1 minute, just to combine. You want the additions to remain intact.

5 Divide the dough into three equal-sized balls and wrap each tightly in plastic wrap. Refrigerate at least 30 minutes or up to overnight.

6 Preheat the oven to 375°F. To shape the scones, flour your counter or cutting board with a light dusting of brown rice flour. Using floured hands, pat the chilled dough ball into an 8-inch round, roughly 1 inch thick. Using a sharp knife or a bench scraper, form the scones. Cut the dough round in half, then cut each half in half (you now have 4 quarters), then cut each quarter in half yet again, forming 8 wedges per round. At this point, you can also freeze the unbaked scones in zip-top bags for up to 1 month. Bake them straight from the freezer, using the baking time and temperature in the recipe.

7 Place the scones on two parchment-lined baking sheets, spaced about 2 inches apart. Brush the scones with the remaining 2 table-spoons heavy cream and sprinkle with a little coarse salt and a few of the reserved nuts. Bake for 18 minutes. Rotate pans and bake another 8–10 minutes, until scones are lightly brown on top and feel just set to the touch. Allow to cool for 10 minutes on the baking sheet before removing.

Fresh scones are best served warm on the day they are made or freeze cooled scones in a zip-top bag for up to 1 month.

SWEET PASTRY DOUGH FOR PIES & TARTS

Every baker needs a go-to pastry dough in their recipe arsenal, and this is it! It's tender and light, with a shortbread-like texture that makes it perfect for all manner of fillings. This is our master recipe for all the pies, galettes, and tarts we make at the bakeshops. Use the rolling instructions provided in the recipe for Pistachio Cream Tart with Raspberries (page 128). One of the beauties of gluten-free dough is there is no need for resting time or overhang as the dough does not shrink back. Make and use this dough right away or store it in the refrigerator or freezer until ready to use. Use any extra bits you have left after rolling to cut out leaf or heart shapes to top your pies. Brush the cut-outs with egg wash and sprinkle with coarse sugar and you have a no-waste and very tasty decoration.

MAKES TWO 12-OUNCE ROUNDS; COOK TIME: 10 MINUTES

Brown rice flour	13.75 oz / 2½ cups
Millet flour	5 oz / 1 cup
Tapioca starch	2.5 oz / ½ cup
White sugar	3.5 oz / ½ cup
Kosher salt	½ tsp
Xanthan gum	½ tsp
Cold butter, cut into 1-inch cubes	8 oz / 2 sticks
Eggs	2 large
Cold water	2 oz / ¼ cup, plus more if needed

1 In the bowl of a food processor fitted with the steel blade, pulse together brown rice flour, millet flour, tapioca starch, sugar, salt, and xanthan gum a few times just to combine. Add the cold butter and pulse again until the butter is the size of small peas, about 30 seconds. Add eggs and continue pulsing until the dough begins to crumble, another 30 seconds or so. Add the cold water all at once and process until the dough comes together. Press the dough together with your fingers. If it holds together, there is no need for more water. If it still feels a bit crumbly, add additional cold water, 1 tablespoon at a time, until the dough feels smooth and holds together well.

2 Shape the dough into two 12-ounce rounds. Wrap in plastic wrap and use immediately, or store in the refrigerator up to 3 days or the freezer up to 1 month.

SAVORY PASTRY DOUGH FOR QUICHE & SAVORY GALETTES

A savory version of my Sweet Pastry Dough for Pies & Tarts (opposite), this recipe will become your go-to for all manner of quiches, savory tarts, galettes, turnovers, hand pies, etc. This recipe makes 2 dough rounds, so use one right away and freeze one for later use. It's light and tender yet stable enough to provide a solid base for every type of filling I've ever put inside. Try it with my Roasted Mushroom, Leek & Gruyère Quiche (page 176).

MAKES TWO 12-OUNCE ROUNDS; COOK TIME: 10 MINUTES

Brown rice flour	13.75 oz / 2½ cups
Millet flour	5 oz / 1 cup
Tapioca starch	2.5 oz / ½ cup
White sugar	1 oz / 2 TB
Kosher salt	1 tsp
Ground black pepper	½ tsp
Xanthan gum	½ tsp
Cold butter, cut into 1-inch cubes	8 oz / 2 sticks
Eggs	2 large
Cold water	2 oz / ¼ cup

1 In the bowl of a food processor fitted with the steel blade, pulse the brown rice flour, millet flour, tapioca starch, sugar, salt, black pepper, and xanthan gum together a few times just to combine. Add the butter and pulse again until the butter is the size of small peas, about 30 seconds. Add the eggs and continue pulsing, until the dough begins to crumble, another 30 seconds or so. Add the cold water all at once and pulse until the dough comes together. Press the dough together with your fingers. If it holds together, there is no need for more water. If it still feels crumbly, add additional cold water, 1 tablespoon at a time, until the dough feels smooth and holds together well.

2 Shape the dough into two 12-ounce rounds. Wrap in plastic wrap and use immediately, or store in the refrigerator up to 3 days or freezer for up to 1 month.

ALL-PURPOSE VEGAN PASTRY DOUGH

My vegan solution to pie crust, this recipe is the result of much trial and error. This lovely dough is tender, full of excellent flavor, easy to work with, and serves as the perfect base for any filling you can throw into it. I was committed to developing a recipe that did not use shortening or margarine, which are the typical vegan go-tos for pie crust. The coconut oil here lends great flavor in a wholesome way. At the bakeries, we use it as a crust for our holiday fruit and summer berry galettes. This crust is minimally sweet, which means you could certainly use it for savory applications as well.

MAKES THREE 12-OUNCE ROUNDS; COOK TIME: 10 MINUTES

Brown rice flour	11 oz / 1 cup
Millet flour	2.5 oz / ½ cup
White rice flour	5 oz / 1 cup
Tapioca starch	2.5 oz / ½ cup
Kosher salt	1 tsp
White sugar	1 TB
Xanthan gum	1 tsp
Coconut oil, at scoopable temperature	5 oz / 1¼ cups
Cold water	13 oz / 1½ cups

1 In the bowl of a stand mixer fitted with the paddle attachment, mix together brown rice flour, millet flour, rice flour, tapioca starch, salt, sugar, and xanthan gum on low speed, just to combine, about 1 minute. Add the scoopable (not melted) coconut oil and mix on low speed again, until the dough resembles coarse meal, 2–3 minutes more. Add the cold water all at once and mix until a dough forms. The dough should hold together well and be smooth. It's ok if small lumps of coconut oil remain in the dough. They will melt when baked, giving the dough more flakiness.

2 Shape the dough into three 12-ounce rounds, wrap in plastic wrap, and refrigerate or freeze until ready to use.

GLOSSARY OF TERMS & INGREDIENTS USED IN THIS BOOK

WHY ARE INGREDIENTS LISTED FIRST?

Yes, I know it's unconventional. But, when I write a recipe I always put the ingredients on the left followed by the quantities on the right. When you're reading a recipe, I think you immediately want to know what's in it, so you can quickly check that you have what you need in your pantry or create a shopping list. To me, this is the most efficient way to organize the information. I hope you'll also find this method helpful and that it simplifies your baking process.

FATS

Baking spray: There are many good brands of baking sprays out there and any that you have easy access to is fine. I typically use a neutral-flavored spray like non-GMO canola. I avoid "butter-flavored" sprays and all other flavored versions, even coconut oil spray, which can impart a coconut flavor to the finished product. The most important thing when choosing a spray is to make sure it sprays a fine, even layer on your pan to ensure that the finished baked good will release easily from the pan. Make sure you read the ingredients on the baking spray before purchasing it, as some contain flour, which is definitely not gluten-free.

Butter, cold: When a recipe calls for "Butter, cold," I mean that your butter should be as cold as possible when you add it to the recipe. This technique is generally called for in order to maintain a flaky texture in a baked item (like a pastry crust or biscuits). When cold butter meets the heat of the oven the

water particles in the butter dissolve to form steam, adding flakiness to the finished product. There are two primary ways to achieve this: 1) Cut your butter into small cubes as soon as you take it out of the fridge, and add it to the mixture as quickly as possible with minimal handling (my preferred method). Or, 2) Cut your butter into small cubes then refrigerate or freeze the cubes before adding them to the mixture. If you're slower on prep this might be the best way for you to achieve the proper "chill" level.

Butter, soft: You'll see many of my recipes call for "Butter, soft." By that I mean your butter should be at soft room temperature before you add it to a batter or dough. It should still hold together and not be melted, unless specified. But, it should be quite soft and spreadable so that it evenly emulsifies when mixed with sugar in a recipe. Unless specifically called for, the butter used in all recipes in this book should be unsalted. I've included a handful of recipes like Salted Butter Chocolate Chip Cookies (page 62) that do use salted butter. But generally speaking, salted or cultured butters should be reserved for eating and spreading on finished items, not for making doughs or batters. Most of my recipes do call for salt as its own ingredient, which allows the baker to control the amount of salt in any given recipe and balance flavors.

Coconut oil: When to use it melted and when to use it solid? Generally in baking we melt coconut oil completely before measuring or using it in a recipe. So, when a recipe calls for "1-cup melted coconut oil" that means you want to scoop out solid oil from the jar, melt it completely, and then measure out precisely 1 cup for your recipe. Melting the oil allows it to be fully combined with the other ingredients. In this book there is one recipe (All-Purpose Vegan Pastry Dough, page 226) that calls for coconut oil "at scoopable temperature," which means cool enough to use in its solid state. In that particular case, the scoopable coconut oil is added and mixed only partially into the dough, resulting in a flakier finished product.

Cream cheese, soft: What exactly do I mean by "cream cheese, soft"? I mean very soft but not melted. When you press down softly, you should be able to push your finger all the way through it. It should cut easily like room temperature butter. You can achieve this by softening the cream cheese in the microwave for about 45 seconds on high setting before using it or by leaving it out on your counter, covered, at room temperature for up to 2 hours.

Vegetable oil: In recipes that call for vegetable oil, I generally use rice bran oil. You can, of course, use canola, safflower, or any neutral-flavored vegetable oil you have on hand. I prefer rice bran oil because it is a by-product of rice production, and therefore sustainably sourced, and adds no detectable flavor to any baked goods. It also has a high smoke point, and is non-GMO. You can find it in most well-stocked specialty food stores or natural foods stores.

FLOURS

Almond meal: You'll see blanched almond meal referenced in many of my recipes. This is readily available in most well-stocked markets, often called almond flour. Look for the blanched variety if you can find it as it adds a lighter color and texture to the finished product.

AP flour blends: Most gluten-free recipes in baking books call for an all-purpose GF flour (i.e., 1 cup gluten-free flour blend). While this may be more convenient, it will not yield the best results across the board. A scone should have a different texture than a cake. Breads should be different from cookies. To achieve that distinct texture in each item, you will need to mix and match various flours with the right amounts of protein and starch. Therefore, you will not find an "all-purpose" gluten-free flour blend in this book. Each recipe requires its own unique flour blend. Yes, that means your pantry will need to be well stocked with a handful of different flours, but this is the art of gluten-free baking. Learning to combine and adjust quantities of various flours will greatly improve your ability to manipulate and control the results of the finished products you bake.

Gluten-free rolled oats: GF oats taste, look, and behave the same as "regular" rolled oats. Why is the gluten-free designation important? Oats are one of those ingredients that are "naturally" gluten-free. However, they are often grown as a rotator crop alternating with wheat in the same fields and therefore

many wheat plants sprout up with the oats and around them. When the oats are harvested, so is the errant wheat and it all gets processed together. Hence "regular" oats can be contaminated with large amounts of wheat. Depending on your sensitivity, look for those that are certified gluten-free, which are grown a certain distance from wheat fields and processed in a certified GF facility. GF oats are typically available right next to the regular oats at most well-stocked markets and natural foods stores. Also important to note here is that oats, whether gluten-free or not, are often heavily sprayed with the herbicide glyphosate (i.e., Roundup). Because of this, choose oats that are gluten-free and organic if available.

Millet flour: I often use millet flour in my recipes as part of my flour blend. A super healthy seed, millet adds protein and starch to recipes. I especially love it for the warm, golden color it imparts to finished baked goods.

Rice flour: There are a variety of rice flours available these days. In this book, I use primarily brown rice flour and white rice flour. Generally they are available in a fine grind, which works well in all my recipes. Avoid sweet rice flour, mochi flour, or coarsely ground rice flours as they will impart a different texture to the finished baked goods. If you're concerned about arsenic levels in your rice, look for flours that are derived from rice grown in California, India, or Pakistan, which typically have significantly lower levels of arsenic than those grown in other regions.

Sorghum flour: There are two types of sorghum flour readily available in most well-stocked natural foods stores "white" sorghum and "natural" sorghum. You want to choose white sorghum whenever possible. Similar to the distinction between white rice and brown rice, it's the grain minus the outer husk ground down into a flour. Using white sorghum results in a more finely textured baked good with a lighter color.

Tapioca starch: A grain-free flour derived from the cassava root, tapioca starch is sometimes sold as tapioca flour. The two are interchangeable so buy whichever you can find at your local store. A staple in my gluten-free pantry, tapioca adds important starch and binding qualities to baked goods. It also adds lightness and a smooth texture. Tapioca can be used as a thickener and is interchangeable in most recipes that call for cornstarch.

Teff flour: Originating from North Africa and the world's smallest seed, teff has a wonderful, nutty quality. Most Americans are familiar with teff from injera, the Ethiopian flatbread, which happens to be naturally gluten-free. Teff is also highly fermentable, making it a natural choice for gluten-free sourdough.

LEAVENERS

Flax eggs: Flaxseed meal "bloomed" in water is a great substitute for eggs in many vegan recipes. A general formula is: 1 flax egg = 1 tablespoon flaxseed meal (golden or brown) + 3 tablespoons water. Stir together and let sit for 5–10 minutes until the flax forms a gel, then add to the recipe as instructed. Flax "eggs" lend a great, springy texture to the finished baked good, which also helps them store well, refrigerated or frozen, for several days. You can use the above formula as a substitute for regular eggs in non-vegan recipes as well.

Instant yeast: What is the difference between using instant yeast and active dry yeast in baking recipes? Active dry yeast is typically used by home bakers and must first be "bloomed" in water before it is added to a recipe. Instant yeast can be added along with the dry ingredients and requires no additional water or "blooming time." I prefer instant yeast as it is more reliably active and produces more consistent results. You can find instant yeast at most well-stocked supermarkets or online. Any extra instant yeast should be kept refrigerated after opening. If you absolutely cannot find instant yeast, you can use active dry. Just swap out ¼ cup of tepid water indicated in the recipe and instead use it to bloom the yeast. If you go the "active dry" route, you will want to add the bloomed yeast with the wet ingredients rather than the dry.

Levain: This term "levain" refers to a pre-ferment used for sourdough items. I use it here for my sourdough bagels (page 165), sourdough loaves (page 210), and sourdough waffles (page 43). Most often, it's a mix of sourdough starter, flour, and water. When mixed together and left to proof, either overnight or for a few hours at room temperature, levain gives extra flavor and helps to create an open texture in the finished bread.

SEASONINGS & FLAVORINGS

Bittersweet chocolate: When I call for "bittersweet" chocolate, I'm looking for a chocolate that contains 64–75 percent cocoa mass. I prefer the South American cacao varietals used by TCHO or El Rey as they're both fair trade and organic and I enjoy their fruity flavor profiles. But use any bittersweet chocolate that you can find that you enjoy the flavor of on its own. Scharffen Berger and Guittard make several varieties that are easily found at most gourmet markets. Whatever you choose, just remember that your finished product will only be as good as the chocolate you start with.

Kosher salt: Kosher salt is a small crystal salt as opposed to iodized or table salt, which has a round, regular shape. I prefer to use kosher salt in baking as it tends to be a little less salty tasting, providing a nice balance to the sweetness of baked goods while not overwhelming you with salty flavor.

Vanilla paste: You'll often see me refer to vanilla paste in my ingredient lists in addition to, or in place of, vanilla extract. Why use vanilla paste? If you're sensitive to grain alcohol, vanilla paste gives you all the vanilla flavor, minus the alcohol. Also, it imparts the appearance of vanilla seeds to the finished product, which is particularly nice in things like icings because it alerts you to the flavor the minute you see the vanilla seeds. What is vanilla paste? It's essentially whole vanilla pods that are ground up with a very small amount of sugar. I like Nielsen Massey vanilla paste for its excellent quality and flavor. It's readily available at most well-stocked supermarkets and specialty stores.

SWEETENERS

Brown sugar: When I call for "brown sugar," I mean golden brown sugar as opposed to dark brown sugar. What is brown sugar exactly? It's essentially white sugar with molasses added. Brown sugar imparts a richer, deeper flavor to baked goods and will enhance the chewiness as well. If all you have on hand is dark brown sugar, you can substitute that in the same quantity, but be aware that it has a higher moisture content so the finished baked goods might be softer/chewier and they will be darker in color.

Coconut sugar: Coconut sugar is a lower glycemic sugar with a distinctly coconut-y flavor. It can be used interchangeably for golden brown sugar in most recipes if you prefer. I generally use Wholesome Sweeteners Coconut Sugar as it is widely available across the country.

Maple syrup: When cooking I always use Grade B maple syrup or Grade A Dark Amber maple syrup; the darker the syrup, the stronger and more pronounced its flavor. Any mid-priced, 100-percent pure maple syrup will do for baking as once it's combined with other ingredients you don't notice the same subtleties that you would if it were drizzled on pancakes or waffles.

White sugar: When I refer to "white sugar," I mean granulated sugar or fine white baker's sugar. My favorite brand for baking, both at home and in my shops, is C&H Baker's Sugar (ultrafine pure cane sugar). I prefer sugar derived from sugarcane, as is typical in the western United States, as opposed to sugar derived from beet sources, as is more common in the eastern United States. Cane sugar is primarily non-GMO as opposed to sugar beets, which in the United States are almost always genetically modified.

THICKENERS

Pectin: A handful of bread recipes in this book call for fruit pectin. In the bakery we use apple pectin, but that can be difficult to find for the home cook. A mixed fruit pectin like Sure-Jell or Pomona's Universal Pectin, both readily available, will work just fine. We use pectin to provide structure in some breads since we don't have the gluten from regular flour to do that for us. It's a more wholesome way to provide some elasticity to breads rather than filling them with starches, gums, and enzymes.

Xanthan gum: What is it? It's a sugar, made from a type of fermented bacteria, typically derived from corn. It is used as a thickening or binding agent in GF baking. Why do we use it? It can mimic the stretching abilities of wheat gluten. In this book I use xanthan gum in moderation, only as much as is needed to achieve the desired texture and structure.

RECIPE INDEX

INDEX

ACKNOWLEDGMENTS

This book has been almost a decade in the making, from concept to publication. I am grateful to so many for their belief in my vision throughout this process, and without whom this project would never have seen the light of day.

My parents, Diane Hardcastle and Robert Hardcastle, who always taught me that I could do whatever I put my mind to. They believed strongly in education and sacrificed to provide me with opportunities. I was always encouraged to follow my passion. Their belief that I should first find what I loved to do, and that I could later figure out how to make my living doing it, was a blessing. It set me down the road of entrepreneurship early and I have never looked back.

My amazing work family. Their belief in Flour Craft and in me as a leader has been steadfast. These good people make me excited to go to work every day. Their positivity and excitement for their work inspires me to work harder every day, knowing that the more our business grows the more I can provide for them and their families. Honestly, there would be no book without their competence in running the show while I was often singularly focused on making this project happen. And they were the magical elves creating most of the food for the photos in this book. My managers, bakers, and cooks (past & present) especially, Elena Suozzi, Mario Zarat, Javier Arias, & Alvaro Ucan. Your creativity, dedication, and work ethic are truly unmatched. I am honored to know you all and to have you on my team. And to all my line cooks, bakers, prep cooks, warewashers, front of house leaders, & baristas . . . It truly takes a village and none of this would be possible without you. Truly.

My teachers and mentors along the way, of which there have been many. From grade school to university, from culinary school to restaurant chefs, business leaders to editors. You have all inspired me to find my own voice along the way and to keep moving the brand ahead. Walter Robb, your belief in Flour Craft from the beginning has been an honor. It is a privilege to call on your experience for advice along the way. Helen Russell, your visionary leadership inspires me daily. Your belief that you can run a thriving business in an ethical way is one I hope to model along my own journey. Danielle Svetcov, literary agent, thank you for believing that this project deserved to happen and for selflessly connecting me to the right people to make it so. Erika Lenkert, thank you for helping me get the wheels of this project off the ground.

My creative team. Being lucky enough to have these amazingly creative women help bring my vision to life has been a dream. How lucky I was to be in your orbits for even a short while. Erin Scott, the masterful photographer and prop stylist behind this gorgeous book, who believed in this project, long before there was even "a project" to believe in. Lillian Kang, the rock-star food stylist behind making all the food look its very best. Thanks for letting me play in your magical world for a week. Nicola Parisi, photo assistant, for all her hustling and her critical eye. Ashley Lima, for the stunningly beautiful and elegant book design. You all make for an inimitable team.

My recipe testers. You all selflessly honed and refined the recipes herein and helped me see the food through fresh eyes. A million thank-yous for your tireless work: Julie Perko-Thomas, Elle Jones, Kielty Nivaud, Leigh Denbo, Susan Lopes, Alexandra Harmer, Kris Ferguson, Ben Lynch, Mairin Chesney, Susan Ginwala, Amy Walsh, Meghan Ellis, Nan Foster, Natalie Kitamura, Marissa Taffer, Taylor Martin, Diane Springfield.

My publishing team from Rizzoli, especially my patient and creative editor, Jono Jarrett, who always pushed me to deliver my best. Jim Muschett, Charles Miers, Colin Hough-Trapp, Lynn Scrabis, Jessica Napp—I couldn't ask for a better team to guide me through my first book.

Last, but certainly not least, my dear husband of twenty-four-plus years, Rick Perko. Without you, this book, our business, the life which we're so blessed to enjoy, would not be possible. You are my rock, my support, my biggest cheerleader, and the most formidable business partner I could ever ask for. How lucky we were to find each other so early in life. I am grateful for every day we get to spend together.

HEATHER HARDCASTLE understood where gourmet gluten free was headed before everyone else. In the early 2000s, diagnosed with gluten intolerance, and passionate about food and cooking, Heather left her well established career and enrolled at the Culinary Institute of America, determined to learn the nuances of great pastry and solid classical technique. Her dream was always to turn her passion and knowledge into a thriving business, creating delicious, high-quality gluten-free baked goods. In 2013, she opened the first Flour Craft Bakery. Today, more than 500 guests line up daily for signature Flour Craft cinnamon rolls, breads, salads, sandwiches, cookies, specialty cakes, and more sold at their cafes. Many of Heather's fans aren't necessarily gluten-free, they just love what she's baking. This is her first cookbook.